No Longer Bound

Peggy Shirley

2020

Cover design by Jeremy Shirley

Table of Contents

Introduction 1
Chapter One
Strongholds: The Chains that Bind 4
Chapter Two
Fear, Worry, and Anxiety 20
Chapter Three
Rejection, Low Self-esteem, Guilt, and Shame 34
Chapter Four
Jealousy 45
Chapter Five
Offense and Bitterness 55
Chapter Six
Lust and Sexual Impurities 65
Chapter Seven
Pride, Rebellion, and Lying 82
Chapter Eight
Anger 92
Conclusion 102

This teaching manual is intended for personal study; however, the author encourages all students to also become teachers and to share the truths from this text with others. However, copying the text itself without permission from the author is considered plagiarism, which is punishable by law. To obtain permission to quote material from this book, please contact:

Peggy Shirley
3210 Cathedral Spires Dr.
Colorado Springs, CO 80904
teachallnations@msn.com
www.teachallnationsmission.com

Introduction

Often, the things we struggle with the most as adults go back to our childhoods. I was just ten years old when I experienced a traumatic situation that haunted me for decades to come. I had written a poem, and my teacher asked me to memorize and recite it at the Parent Teacher Association meeting. I had never done anything like that, but I thought it would be easy. However, when I got up to speak, it seemed like millions of eyes were staring at me. Confusion and fear swept over my mind. When I opened my mouth to speak, those staring eyes chased away every syllable I had so diligently memorized. My mind froze, and I stood there speechless until tears began to fill my eyes and I ran off the stage. Backstage, safe from those glaring eyes, I made a vow to never again speak in public.

From that vow, I developed a stronghold—a controlling negative emotion—of fear that stopped me from public speaking for many years. When opportunities to speak publicly would arise, I had a strong sensation that I was going to be sick to my stomach or that something terrible would happen. I hated every minute of public speaking. As an adult, I felt led by the Lord to preach the Gospel, but unfortunately, my fears hindered me in this calling.

Fear is just one of the strongholds that I have dealt with in my life. The truth is that strongholds can trouble us even after we become born-again Christians. I know this to be true personally because, after I became a Christian, I continued to experience frustration with negative actions and beliefs. I did not realize that those actions and beliefs could be changed. I believed the lie that I could never get free from them. As challenging as those strongholds were, I suffered with even more strongholds operating in my life that I couldn't see. Sadly, this is the case with most Christians as well.

I am writing this book because I was a victim of strongholds. I know the power they hold over us, but I also know the victory in getting set free from strongholds. In this book, I'll explain exactly what a stronghold is. I'll also discuss sixteen common strongholds and the actions associated with them. Throughout the book, I intend to base all my teaching on what the Bible has to say on each stronghold. Unless otherwise designated, the scriptures in this book are taken from the Amplified Bible. I'll share my personal experiences as well, and I hope that, through my testimony and teaching, many people will be set free. This teaching began in my personal process of finding freedom from my own strongholds but has grown into God's purpose and plan for myself and for others—something that I never could have imagined in my initial breakthrough. I believe this teaching will give you the keys from the Word of God to set you free. You will not only learn to recognize various strongholds, you will also be given the steps to take to pull those strongholds down and the keys to unlock the chains that bind you spiritually and emotionally.

I'm thrilled to say that I have been a minister, teacher, and missionary for over forty years. I've seen the Lord break many strongholds—not only for me, but for the people I have counseled or taught in classes on pulling down strongholds. Even though I was bound for many years by the stronghold that began as a ten-year-old child, today, I speak in front of hundreds of people each year and actually look forward to public speaking. If I had never overcome the strongholds in my life, I would not have fulfilled my destiny to become an ordained minister, teacher, and missionary.

God has a plan for your life as well. You have a God-given destiny to fulfill. However, the enemy wants to keep you from your destiny and, instead, have you bound up in the chains of strongholds. I have led mission teams for years. The people on my teams love the Lord and want to be used to teach, heal, and deliver others. However, on repeated trips, I have seen that many of these dear Christians were bound up and chained to the past. Opportunities would arise for members on the teams to help others get set free, but because they were still chained up to the past, they couldn't. Many succumbed to fears and were afraid to speak or testify in front of the people we visited in foreign countries. Fear and low self-esteem had them terrified, when in reality they were good speakers. Unfortunately, fear wasn't the only stronghold to come out during those trips. Jealousy, rebellion, and many other negative actions which caused these team members to fall short of fulfilling the purpose God had in mind for them were exposed.

However, I want you to take heart because those strongholds can be broken. Since learning the principles to pulling down strongholds and teaching them to others, my mission teams have been far more successful. And, through the years, I have marveled at how differently I now act and think because I have taken those strongholds captive. What the Lord has done in my life and in the lives of my mission teams and hundreds of others to whom I've taught these principles, He'll do in your life as well.

Are you ready to eliminate the negative behaviors and thoughts that are holding you back? I invite you to read this book. I promise that your life will never be the same.

One last thing before we begin is that I want you to know that it is my prayer that our sweet Jesus will show you the areas where He wants to break the chains of strongholds in your life. Hosea 4:6 says that God's people are destroyed through their lack of knowledge, but John 8:32 says that you will know the truth from reading the Word, and it will set you free. I speak freedom in all areas of your life where you are bound.

Chapter One
Strongholds: The Chains that Bind

What are strongholds?

Imagine a chain. It is an inanimate object without any kind of inherent power of its own—right? But watch what happens as someone **takes the chain, wraps it around an object, and then secures** a lock through two links of the chain. It may be occurring to you now that the chain cannot be unlocked unless someone has the key; and you're correct, without the key, the chain cannot be released. Now, imagine a believer bound to a chain of fear or anger or any other of a number of negative thoughts. The chain of negative thoughts has been locked into place. People, including believers do their best to "control" themselves, but they struggle under the bondage of the chain. This struggle often results in outbursts of negative emotions and setbacks in life. The negative emotion or bad habit takes control of the person. The invisible chains wrapped around them are binding them and keeping them from freedom in Christ.

This analogy represents what a stronghold is: a chain that binds us to a set of negative thoughts, beliefs, and behaviors. Like a heavy chain, a stronghold is a force or influence that chokes or suppresses freedom of movement or expression. If strongholds are established as thought patterns or emotional responses, they can lead to vain imaginations about yourself, other people, or situations. Strongholds can take control of your responses, place limits on you, and dominate your life. You and you only have the "key" that can release these chains and strongholds with the Lord's help.

Recognizing strongholds

Have you ever been in a situation where you wished you wouldn't have said or done a certain something? Even though you knew what you had done or said was wrong, did something seem to compel you at that moment to act in a way you didn't want to? I think almost everyone can answer "yes" to that question, at least at one time or another. However, if consistent, negative patterns of thought and behavior emerge that you cannot seem to break, you most likely have a stronghold, with an ungodly mindset operating in your life.

It can take some searching to uncover your strongholds. Often, we have become so used to them and are blinded to them that God will have to use other people to help us see them. Some of the strongholds that I have eliminated from my life began with my not even seeing that they existed. I had to be willing to hear my husband and friends when they told me of things I was doing or believing that they could see as unhealthy controlling patterns—strongholds.

Examples of strongholds

Strongholds come in many forms. I am amazed at how many people who seem to "have it all together" have many secret strongholds that are negatively controlling or affecting them. Negative words said to them or hurtful things done to them have wrapped them in chains that bind them to their past experiences.

Once, a woman who had been unable to have restful sleep for years came to one of my classes on pulling down strongholds. After sitting through the class, she asked God to show her why she was unable to sleep. Suddenly she realized that it had to do with a long-term trauma from her childhood – almost every night, her father would hide under her bed waiting for her to come to bed so he could rape her. When she thought back on those experiences – as horrible as they were – she decided that she was not going to let them control her life anymore. After prayer and counsel, she realized how pointless it was to allow something that had happened years before and miles away to continue to control her life. So, she determined to forgive him and be freed from the ongoing effects of the trauma. That night after praying with me, she slept restfully for the first time in years. The chain that bound her had been broken!

On another occasion, a man from my class was suffering with very low self-esteem and little confidence because his father constantly belittled him when he was a young boy. As we talked, I showed him in the Bible what his heavenly Father thought about him. It did take some time and a deliberate program of meditating on scriptures that speak of our identity in Christ, but he eventually began to get a new self-image.

Just like those two individuals experienced new freedom when they confronted their strongholds, we will discover as we go through the lessons in this book that there are many other strongholds – such as rejection, anger, lust, and pride – that place limitations on our lives and result in unhealthy and destructive thinking about ourselves and others. But most importantly – we will learn how to deal with them and overcome them!

Where do strongholds originate?

Although the negative emotions and behaviors that come from strongholds are very real and present to the individuals experiencing them, some are actually imaginations and are not based in truth. Those thoughts come from lies, false beliefs, negative experiences, and words spoken to or about them.

Many people who believe in God as the Creator believe He knew their futures. Jeremiah 29:11 supports this, *For I know the thoughts and plans that I have for you, says the Lord, thoughts and plans for welfare and peace and not for evil, to give you hope in your final outcome.* Christians from many different backgrounds are comfortable with the thought that God knows them and has a future for them.

God knows your future, but He also knows that Satan has a plan for your life. The devil's life's goal is to hurt you, defeat you, and put you in mental chains. The Bible states it this way, *The thief comes only in order to steal and kill and destroy. I came that they may have and enjoy life, and have it in abundance [to the full, till it overflows].* (John 10:10) It is the enemy who comes and tries to bind us with lies and wrong thinking. He tries to direct us (our lives) to what he wants us to believe about life, other people, and ourselves. The battle is a spiritual one, as explained in 2 Corinthians 10:3-5:*For though we walk in the flesh, we do not war after the flesh: (For the weapons of our warfare are not carnal, but mighty through God to the pulling down of **strong holds**;) Casting down imaginations, and every high thing that exalteth itself against the knowledge of God, and bringing into captivity every thought to the obedience of Christ.*

Many of us believe that once we are born again, Satan no longer has a role in our lives. However, in 1 Peter 5:8 Peter wants us to understand that we are at war with an opponent: *Be sober [well balanced and self-disciplined], be alert and cautious at all times. That enemy of yours, the devil, prowls around like a roaring lion [fiercely hungry], seeking someone to devour.* Many of us, even if we were taught about God, are often not taught much about our enemy or his impact on people. We don't realize that, through the lies of our enemy, we have strongholds that have crept in through bad experiences or wrong responses in conflict situations.

We tend to think our actions, thoughts, and behaviors are normal—that they are just a part of who we are, part of our personality. However, as previously mentioned, they are sometimes based on lies from the enemy. John 8:44 tells us, *Satan is the father of all lies and all that is false.* Our enemy will take your bad experiences, including those from your childhood and plant those lies inside you.

Such experiences as the stories I have mentioned are real and are traumatic. However, if you know the Lord, He can heal you and you can have power over any stronghold that might develop. The trouble comes when we don't know the Lord and His Word. This gives Satan the opportunity to come in with negative emotions, lies, and constant reminders of the traumas, failures, or other unfortunate events in our pasts.

Strongholds are acquired when you believe the devil's lies instead of the Bible's truth. When that happens, you begin to oppose or fight the truth. For example, I fought the truth that I was perfectly capable of speaking publicly. I believed the lie that this was something I could never do. I succumbed to irrational fears, rather than walking in the truth of what God said about me and my abilities. Opposition to truth opens us up to vain imaginations. When you become comfortable with your thoughts and actions even though they may be contrary to biblical truth, you are on shaky ground.

How a stronghold grows and takes root in your life...take care of that cavity

How do strongholds develop into controlling behaviors? Let me explain it this way; imagine you notice a sensitivity with one of your teeth, the beginning of a cavity. If you don't deal with it quickly as a small cavity, eventually it can cause a situation that requires a root canal or, worse yet, the extraction of the entire tooth. If you had just addressed the sensitivity in that tooth when the problem was just starting, you could have saved the tooth and yourself from a lot of pain. The same principle applies to a stronghold. If we don't take our problems to the Lord and deal with them when we first notice them, they only deepen and become stronger and more visible. Eventually, they not only damage us, but can damage those around us as well.

The Keys to Demolishing Strongholds

You may be wondering how you can possibly get rid of the strongholds that are binding you? I have great news for you. It can be done. As I explained previously, 2 Corinthians 10:3-5 tells us that it is possible to demolish or destroy those mindsets. Through the rest of this chapter, I'll show you the three essential steps that it takes to pull down strongholds. Although it may take some time, pulling down strongholds is well worth the effort!

Step One: Recognize and acknowledge the strongholds in your life

The first step in pulling down strongholds is to acknowledge them. If you never acknowledge the patterns of negative thoughts and behaviors, you can never deal with them. In other words, you must first "own" that a mindset or stronghold is influencing you.

We can see the importance of realizing our shortcomings through the example of King David in the Bible. When King David became aware of his wrong attitude, he prayed to His Creator to help him overcome it. In Psalm 51:10 KJV, David says, *Create in me a clean heart, O God, and see if there be any hurtful way in me.* Like David, you, too, can ask God to search your heart. Consider your thoughts and actions. Do you experience jealousy when someone receives something you were hoping for? Is anger hard to control when things don't go the way you had hoped? This list of questions could go on and on.

No army in history has ever **conquered** an enemy they were not willing to **confront** on a battlefield. You can win this battle, but you must begin by facing your enemy.

Strongholds and Pride

One of the most deceptive elements to strongholds is that often everyone else can see them in us, but we cannot see them ourselves. I believe this is because of our pride. In this context, pride refers to selfishness or self-deception. We think everyone else has a problem, but not us. We believe that our thoughts and actions are normal and acceptable. This self-deception gives us tunnel vision in which we simply are unable to see that we have allowed strongholds to control our behavior. This type of pride is at the center of every wrong mindset and stronghold.

Pride causes people to be in denial regarding strongholds. You may say, "Well, I've gotten along just fine with thinking this way so far." But I want you to understand, you have just touched the deceptive nature of a stronghold. The lie is that the negative patterns that are holding you back from all that God has for you—in your calling, your relationships, in every area of your life—are just a normal part of who you are. While you are in denial, however, your strongholds are obvious to others, particularly your loved ones.

I experienced this personally. When I got married, my husband really got to see not only my good but also my "not so good" side. Because of experiences in my past, I had a sensitivity to rejection that I hung on to. I never thought I could get rid of it because of all the things that had happened to me. I'll discuss rejection as a stronghold in depth later in this book, but for now you just need to know that I kept experiencing rejection over and over again. Rejection was so much a part of my experience that I took it with me wherever I went. If one of my friends didn't call me back, I thought she was rejecting me when, in reality, she was just busy. I was overly sensitive, which led to low self-esteem.

My husband finally told me one day that I was viewing experiences as rejection that were not meant as rejection. He explained to me that I had a stronghold—a spirit of rejection. After he confronted me about this several times, I finally asked the Lord if what my husband was saying was true. Remember, the Lord is our Father and best friend. He wants to help and heal us. When I asked Him what He thought, He began to show me that my husband was right.

So, step one for me was to move past pride, listen to what my husband said, and "own" and acknowledge that I needed to be set free from a stronghold of rejection.

While at times some strongholds must be pointed out to us by our friends and family, at other times we are able to perceive our own strongholds. For example, I've had to recognize in myself and deal with a fear of public speaking. The first step I took in pulling down this stronghold was acknowledging that the fear and panic I experienced in regard to public speaking were not normal. I had to understand that my emotional reaction was an overreaction.

Although acknowledging a stronghold may take place in a moment, emotional healing takes time. Getting past pride and recognizing your strongholds is a crucial first step, but it is just the beginning.

Key #1: The first step in demolishing a stronghold is to acknowledge that it exists.

Step Two: Face the past and find the root of the stronghold

Once you've recognized your stronghold, the second step in pulling it down is to face the past. You need to get to the root of when a particular stronghold entered your life. Only after realizing the stronghold's entry point can you then effectively remove it from your life. Just as a weed must be pulled up from the root or it will grow back, you have to remove the root of the stronghold to prevent it from resurfacing in our lives. I personally experienced that problem with my driving. Every time I had to turn left without a left turn arrow to clearly give the right of way, I would tense up and get nervous. I dreaded all left turns. One day, my son, noticing my anxiety, asked me why I became so uptight when I had to turn left. I said, "Well, doesn't everybody?" He responded, "No, Mom. You just need to relax." I thought, "Impossible!"

After having him point out that my reaction was not normal, I took my anxiety to the Lord, and He showed me exactly why this stronghold of fear controlled me every time I had to turn left without a left turn arrow. Years ago, I had to turn left at a traffic light that did not have a left turn signal and got stuck in the intersection. I expected oncoming traffic to stop at the red light. An oncoming car didn't stop and hit my car and almost totaled it. However, the police officer on the scene informed me that the main problem with the accident was that I should have stayed back in the turn lane, instead of pulling out into the intersection to turn. I ended up getting a ticket, not the man who ran the red light. I left the scene very shaken by the experience.

After the Lord brought this incident to my memory, I gained insight into where the unnecessary panic came from—this accident that happened years ago came from my failure to follow a safe procedure. Recognizing the root helped me to pull this stronghold down. Now, I have no problems or fears with turning left. When I drive, I know to stay in the turn lane instead of the intersection even during heavy traffic flow to help ensure safety.

I've already talked about the overwhelming fear of public speaking I once had. I want to revisit that story to point out the significance of realizing how that stronghold was able to begin in my life. I had to stop and ask the Lord what was causing the fear I felt when I was asked to speak in front of a crowd. When I finally asked this question, God took me back to the memory of the PTA meeting when I was just ten years old, trying to recite my poem, but instead panicking before all those glaring eyes in front of me. I made a vow to never again speak in public. The Lord showed me that it was that painful moment in grade school that was the root of this stronghold in my life. After recognizing the root, I understood why I felt such negative emotions every time I had to speak publicly; I was reliving that trauma from my grade school years! I realized that the incident happened years ago and that it was over but could see that it was still operating undetected in the background.

Jesus sympathizes with your hurts

Facing the past or admitting a problem area is not always easy. But, thankfully, we have a High Priest who understands and loves us unconditionally. As Hebrews 4:15 says, *For we do not have a High Priest who is unable to <u>understand</u>, <u>sympathize</u>, and have a <u>shared feeling</u> with our <u>weaknesses</u> and <u>temptations</u>, but One who has been tempted in every respect as we are, yet without sin.* Jesus truly understands what we are going through. Remember how the twelve apostles **abandoned** Jesus the night He was to be led to His crucifixion? Remember how Judas **betrayed** Him for money and His dear friend Peter **denied** that he had even known Him? Jesus was **lied about**, **rejected**, and even **crucified**. Isaiah 53:3 says, "He was **despised**, **rejected,** and **forsaken** by men, a man of **sorrows**, **pains**, and **acquainted with grief** and sickness; and like One from whom men hid their faces, He was despised and we did not appreciate His worth or have any esteem for Him." It is important to remember that Jesus came to heal you not only physically, but emotionally as well.

Even Jesus had hurts that He had to leave in the past. The important thing for you to realize is that you hold the key to getting past your past, which is why in Philippians 3:13, God tells us to, forget the things which are behind us. You've got to face the past, but you cannot stay in the past. In life, I've learned that there are three laws of time:

1. Yesterday is history; you can't change it.
2. Today is a present. Enjoy it.
3. Tomorrow is a mystery. Look forward to it with expectation.

Don't defend your actions

Another part of coming to terms with your strongholds is to stop defending your negative actions by saying things such as, "I can't help it," or "That's the way my parents acted." You've got to get past that attitude. Your parents may not have been perfect, but you're not trapped by the mistakes they made. I've experienced this personally. My mother was critical of me all the time. Can you guess what I caught myself hopelessly doing with my own children? I found myself criticizing them unnecessarily. To begin to pull down this stronghold, I had to move past blaming the example that my mother set and ask the Lord to take away the critical spirit in me. After I prayed, this criticism didn't instantly stop, but every time I heard myself starting to criticize, I felt an immediate conviction to stop my complaining.

Key #2: The second key to demolishing a stronghold is to find the root of how it entered your life.

Once you've acknowledged your strongholds and how they are holding you back in life, and you've faced the past to discover the root of how these strongholds came into your life, you are ready for the next step, which is to allow the Holy Spirit to change the way you think about yourself. Proverbs 23:7 says that as a man thinks in his heart, so is he. In other words, what you think about yourself is how you will act.

Step Three: Use the Word of God to renew your mind

Sometimes, Christians don't move into this transformational step because of the incorrect way that they think about their born-again experience. It's important to know the truth about this. When you were saved, your **spirit** was redeemed and saved instantly, but your **soul**—which is your mind, will, and emotions—was not redeemed instantaneously. You have to work on changing your thoughts, actions, and habits. You can do this, as the Bible says in Romans 12:2, by *not being conformed to this world, but being transformed by the renewing of our minds*. This happens when we read and meditate on the truth which is in the Word. Since strongholds are built upon errors and lies, it is through the truth of the Bible that we can change our thought patterns and actions.

Remember, strongholds are built when you accept the devil's lies instead of the biblical truth. You let your negative experiences and emotions—rather than the Word of God—define you. Remember, when that happens, we begin to oppose the truth and open ourselves to vain imaginations. The good news is that meditating and studying what God says about your thoughts and actions can change you. He wants us not to just be "hearers only" of the Word, but "doers" of the Word as well (James 1:22). In other words, you need to let your thoughts and actions line up with the way He wants you to talk and act.

Consider Ephesians 4:22 which tells us to strip ourselves of our former nature, by putting off and discarding our old unrenewed self—this means anything which characterized your previous manner of life and has become corrupt through lusts and desires that spring from delusion. You must be constantly renewed in the spirit of your mind and put on the new nature (the regenerate self) created in God's image in true righteousness and holiness.

Watch your words

When you ask the Lord to change your thinking, you also need to watch the words you speak. Proverbs 6:2 NKJV says, *You are snared by the words of your mouth; You are taken by the words of your mouth*. The power of your words is mentioned again in Proverbs 18:21, "*Death and life are in the power of the tongue and they who indulge in it shall eat the fruit of it.*"

A well-known quote from Mahatma Gandhi captures the power of words very well: *You need to watch your **thoughts** for they become your **words**. Watch your **words**, for they become your **actions**.*

*Watch your **actions**, for they become your **habits**. Watch your **habits** for they become your **character**. Watch your **character**, for it becomes your **destiny**.*

This quote captures a true progression about the power of words and reflects the biblical truth of Proverbs 6:2 and Proverbs 18:21.

We would all do well if we followed Jesus' example. He used the Word and watched His own words when tempted by Satan. Luke 4:3 says that Jesus was hungry after fasting for 40 days and Satan tempted him by saying, *If You are the Son of God, command this stone to turn into bread."* In Luke 4:4, *Jesus replied to him, "It is written and forever remains written, 'Man shall not live by bread alone."* Luke 4:5 goes on to say that the devil promised Jesus the kingdoms of the world and authority over them if Jesus would worship him, but Jesus replied to him again with the Word of God, saying in Luke 4:7, *"You shall worship the Lord your God and serve only Him."* Jesus was then tempted a third time, but He again used the Word; finally, Satan gave up.

This is exactly what we need to do when we are faced with situations, such as when we feel we cannot do something. The Word says this in Philippians 4:13, *I can do all things [which He has called me to do] through Him who strengthens and empowers me [to fulfill His purpose—I am self-sufficient in Christ's sufficiency; I am ready for anything and equal to anything through Him who infuses me with inner strength and confident peace.]* If you feel confused or can't figure out a problem yourself, quote the Word to yourself. Remember that 1 Corinthians 2:16 tells us that we have the mind of Christ—the One who spoke the truth of Scripture and rejected Satan's lies.

Although changing the orientation of a well-established way of thinking can seem insurmountable when you start, as you renew your mind and begin to believe and speak what the Word says, your words, thoughts, and actions will start to change. It takes time and patience to change the course of something that has gone in a set direction over an extended period of time. So be patient during the process. Continually repeating the truth in God's Word will work over time.

Declare the stronghold is over and proclaim the truth

When I first had to speak in public, and the fear, worry, and anxiety strongholds would cause me to tense up, as I previously described, I would pray, "Lord, you have not given me a spirit of fear, but of power, love, and a sound mind." This stronghold has been broken by the power of the blood of Jesus Christ and the Word of God. The root of the stronghold has been discovered and destroyed and the stronghold no longer has control over me, for when the darkness comes to the light, it must go. Lord, you came to set me free and with your help and your words, this will be a great meeting." This is an example of what you might pray to help you embrace truth in your life and speak victory over a stronghold

Allow Jesus to restore you

Remember how in step one—admitting you have a stronghold—we learned that Jesus sympathizes with our hurts? In addition to sympathizing with you, Jesus can also restore you. Jesus suffered all pain so that you would not have to. Do not let your heart keep you in bondage. Jesus can restore what Satan did to you. When I think back over my past and the many pains and disappointments I experienced, I am amazed at how faithful God has been to heal me. Even though what I went through is nothing compared to what some people have gone through, to Him, you and I are all the same. We are His dear children whom He loves and wants to restore.

In Joel 2:25, God gives us an amazing promise: *"And I will restore or replace for you the years that the locust* (Satan) *has eaten."* All you need to do is cooperate in the way He has made for your freedom, allowing Jesus to heal your hurts. Take your sorrows to Jesus who will heal you.

The truth will set you free

John 8:32 says, *And you will know the Truth and the Truth will set you free.* You need to purpose in your heart to choose your thoughts and words carefully. When I began to work on my strongholds—such as rejection and fear—and began to speak the Word when a negative thought came against me, I started to get free. I learned that I could strip myself of my former nature as Ephesians 4:22-24 tells us to do.

God has renewed my mind concerning many strongholds, including my fear of public speaking. After recognizing this fear as a stronghold in my life, and then discovering that it entered my life through my grade school experience, I was ready to renew my mind. I renounced and broke the words I had spoken over myself when I vowed I would never again speak in public. After continually speaking the Word in this area of my life and with time and practice, public speaking and teaching went from being fearful experiences to rewarding opportunities that I look forward to! If I had not faced that fear and asked the Lord to help me take those thoughts captive, I would not have fulfilled the call on my life to become an ordained minister and missionary.

Key #3 The third key is to renew your mind through the Word and allow God to restore you.

Although our enemy seems powerful, the fight is "fixed" in our favor if we will train and use the weapons we have been given in Christ. God has given us power to defeat Satan through Jesus. Second Corinthians 10:3-5 KJV tells us for strongholds to be removed, we must do our part. Read the verse again: *For though we walk in the flesh, we do not war after the flesh: (For the weapons of our warfare are not carnal, but mighty through God to the* **pulling down of strong holds;) Casting down imaginations, and every high thing that exalteth itself against the knowledge of God***, and bringing into captivity every thought to the obedience of Christ.* **We** must demolish strongholds through the spiritual authority **we** have been given. We must take negative thoughts captive and align them with the Word of God. If we refuse what the Bible says, we will remain bound to the enemy's wrong thinking and lies.

Why we need to pull down strongholds...a vision

One day, God gave me a vision of His end-time army. I believe this vision gets to the very core of the vital importance of why Christians need to pull down their strongholds. In this vision, God's army was divided into three groups. The first group consisted of those trying to enlist but were unable to pass the physical exam because of past wounds and negative strongholds. This group was still in God's school. They would never flunk out because God is willing to deal with them again and again—all the way until they master the material. But they weren't yet ready to join the army despite their desire to do so.

The second group in God's army included those in spiritual boot camp being trained for God's service by letting Him begin to heal them, change them, and develop them into godly warriors. This group was building their spiritual muscles. As Psalm 23:3 KJV says, He restoreth my soul: He leadeth me in the paths of righteousness for His name's sake. This group was being restored by God and strengthened in Him. They were in the last steps before being ready to live and fight for God.

The third group of people in God's army were those in active duty. They weren't holding on to strongholds, they submitted to spiritual training through God's Word, they spent time with the Lord and continued to do so, and now they were ready for battle. Being ready does not mean being perfect. Let me be clear, the people in this group were not perfect, God doesn't use **perfect** vessels; instead, He uses **purified** vessels. His promise to us is *that He who has begun a good work in you will [continue to] perfect and complete it until the day of Christ Jesus [the time of His return]*. (Philippians 1:6) The people in this group were not perfect, but they were ready.

The truth is that all of us are in the refining process. To purify gold, it is put into a crucible and heated up. Gold is heavy, so it goes to the bottom of the pot. The other impure metals float to the top of the crucible and are skimmed off. Life is like our crucible. If we allow God to purify us, as the piece of gold He sees us as, the impurities in our life will slowly rise to the surface so they can be removed. This process is described in Malachi 3:3: *He will sit as a refiner and purifier of silver, and He will purify the sons of Levi (the priests), and refine them like gold and silver, so that they may present to the Lord (grain) offerings in righteousness.*

Satan will try to deceive and tell you that there are no areas that need to be worked on or refined in your life. That is simply another one of his lies.

Believing those lies will stop you from living in God's best and fulfilling your destiny. Are you ready to shake Satan's lies from your life? The keys to doing so is within your reach!

Chapter Two
Fear, Worry, and Anxiety

My stomach was in knots as I sat in bed. I couldn't possibly go to sleep with the situation that was on my heart. My youngest son and a friend were going snowmobiling. This usually wouldn't have caused me to worry enough to wake up, but the news channels had just announced that evening that several dangerous avalanches had just struck in the area where my son was going. To make matters worse, I had a stronghold of fear that I was working on pulling down. Because of this stronghold of fear, vain imaginations began to form in my mind. Fear began to dominate me and cause me to feel great distress. I became overwhelmed with a feeling of doom that something terrible would happen to my son.

If worry leads to prayer, it can become a good thing. The Bible tells us clearly that God can deliver us from all our fears if we seek Him (Psalm 34:4). This can lead to a trust, a peace, and a rest. God knows that we are going to have problems in this life. He says in 1 Peter 5:7 to cast the entirety of our cares, anxieties, worries, and concerns on Him. Why? Because God cares for us—and He cares for us watchfully—so that's why we give our worries over to the Lord.

Remembering these things led me to recognize that I was allowing fear to control me when I thought about the situation with my son's going snowmobiling. So, I began to cast my cares upon the Lord. I began to lift up my son and his friend in prayer. I began to command peace upon myself and for angels to surround my son. Then, I said, "Lord, "I'm going to go to sleep now and I trust you with my son." And the next thing I knew, my son came home with no problems.

Unfortunately, this is not the only example of the stronghold of fear operating in my life—I've had several other experiences which I'll share with you in this chapter. These fears kept me from living in God's freedom, and they'll stop you, too, if you don't remove them.

Understanding fear, worry, and anxiety

Fear, worry, and anxiety are three common strongholds which most people have struggled with in their lives. These three are interconnected and affect one another. It tends to be a vicious cycle. Fear sets in, and we begin to worry. As worry grows, it may develop into an all-consuming anxiety. Tragically, many people's lives are controlled by not just one, but two, or even all three.

So, just what are fear, worry, and anxiety? The Greek word for **fear** is *phobos*, which means phobia, dread, and terror. Webster's Dictionary defines fear as a painful feeling of impending danger, anxiety, foreboding, or panic. **Worry** is defined as mental distress or agitation resulting from concern, usually for something impending or anticipated. Finally, **anxiety** is defined as apprehensive uneasiness or nervousness, usually over an impending or anticipated ill; and medically as "an abnormal and overwhelming sense of apprehension and fear often marked by physical signs (such as tension, sweating, and increased pulse rate) and by self-doubt about one's capacity to cope with it." Some of the key words in these definitions are abnormal, overwhelming, distress, agitation, and nervousness.

Therefore, fear, worry, and anxiety are negative emotions that we develop as an overreaction to concern. Strongholds of fear, worry, and anxiety go beyond the discomfort that often comes with new situations, but are controlling emotions that limit people in what they believe they can and cannot do. Fear, worry, and anxiety set boundaries in a person's life that God never intended to exist.

Spirit, soul, and body

In Chapter One, I explained how we are attacked in our souls. A proper understanding of spirit, soul, and body is incredibly important to removing strongholds from our lives.

Let's consider the concept of spirit, soul, and body more

closely. All throughout recorded human history, people have referred to the seen part of a person as the body and the unseen part as the soul. The soul was considered the part that feels (emotions) and knows (intellect) things. The body was the house of the personality. In most cultures, it was believed that in death the soul left the body. When the unseen part of a person departs from the body, the body is considered dead. Although most cultures without Christ acknowledge body and soul, the Bible says that we are actually triune beings—like the Godhead. In 1 Thessalonians 5:23, Paul prays for believers to be preserved until Christ's return in their spirits, souls, and bodies: *And the very God of peace sanctify you wholly; and I pray God your whole spirit and soul and body be preserved blameless unto the coming of our Lord Jesus Christ.*

After understanding that we are three-part beings, we next need to see the relationships among spirit, soul, and body and how the enemy attacks us. It is your soul—your mind, will, and emotions—that Satan attacks with his lies. In contrast, your born-again spirit is alive to God. If you feel anxious, fearful, have physical pain (such as headaches, stomach aches, or chest pains) accompanying your feelings of fear, you are being attacked in your soul, not your spirit.

This attack in your soul may next affect your body. According to Caroline Leaf in her book, *Who Switched Off My Brain*, fear triggers more than fourteen hundred known chemical and physical responses and activates more than thirty different hormones and neurotransmitters. What started in your soul becomes an intense emotional and physical reaction.

Fear may seem invisible and not as real as a danger that you can see, but fear is dangerous because it drains you and keeps you from doing things you are destined to do, going to the places you are destined to go to, and saying the things you are destined to say. Like the fictional Superman who could perform tremendous feats of strength and energy—yet became powerless when near Kryptonite—fear robs us of strength and energy as well. Kryptonite made Superman weak and useless, and fear is literally our Kryptonite. It leads to worry and anxiety. The Bible sums up the force of fear in 1 John 4:18 KJV, *fear hath torment.*

Examples of fear

Most of the examples of fear that we see are not founded in reality. The commonly known acrostic for fear—**F**alse **E**vidence **A**ppearing **R**eal—is true. The vast majority of our fears never happen! I know people who are afraid to fly, when the reality is they are safer in a plane than in a car. I know adults who are terrified of dogs because as a child they were bitten by one. For example, we once had a man from another country visiting at our house. This man was a leader in his church and was usually a rational and confident man. We hoped to have a pleasant visit, but unfortunately, when he saw my son's dog, he froze in fear. His panic consumed him until he finally ran up the stairs, saying he wouldn't come down until the dog left. My son couldn't understand how a grown man could act so childishly. My son's dog was very well-behaved and not a threat to anyone. It turned out that the country the man was from allows dogs to run wild, and he had once been bitten by one of the wild dogs. The man's negative experiences from childhood led him to develop a stronghold of fear which caused him to shrink back in fear any time he was around a dog.

Personally, I'm trying to get over the fear of mice. For whatever reason, when I see a mouse, I panic and scream. You'd think a real terror had entered the room. The tiny little mouse certainly has more reason to be afraid of me than I am of it. I am working on this, but it's just a simple example of something that upsets lots of people and of how fears are not based in truth yet affect many people.

Another fear I am pushing out of my life is the fear of heights. To help with this, my husband once made me go on one of the country's highest Ferris wheels. I did it with many screams and a few, "get me off this now!" demands, but I survived. And, I realized nothing bad had happened to me. It was all a senseless core of anxiety.

I also must deal with fears during my travels around the world as a missionary. I go to many foreign countries where all is quite different from the United States, and I don't know their language or customs. Many, many times, the enemy tries to make me think I don't have what it takes to be an effective teacher in these countries—that my teachings aren't good or that the people won't understand me. Then he attacks me with endless "what ifs", such as "What if the flight crashes and I never see my husband or three sons again?" All these thoughts are False Evidence Appearing Real. So, what do I do with my fears? I take them to the Lord. He always says to me, "There you go again trying to do it on your own talents and strengths." And then He says to me, "I will be with you, Peggy. Everywhere you go and in everything you do." Then, I read scriptures on fear, and I always get comforted, and my confidence comes back. This is what I encourage you to do as well when you are attacked with fear.

Are you beginning to see how fears control us? Can you see their effect on our choices and behaviors? We need to talk about our fears and begin to face them.

Where does fear come from?

Where is fear from? Second Timothy 1:7 KJV makes it clear that fear is not from God: *For God hath not given us a spirit of fear but of love, power, and a sound mind.* The Amplified Bible says, *but [He has given us a spirit] of power and of love and of sound judgment and personal discipline [abilities that result in a calm and well-balanced mind and discipline and self-control.* Clearly, fear is not from God, but rather is an attack from the enemy who wants to keep us from all God has for us. Fear is Satan's tool to bind and keep you miserable. It drains you and keeps you from fulfilling your destiny.

Step One: Confronting and admitting your fears

Praise God, I have been set free from the stronghold of fear—and you can be set free too. Pulling down the strongholds of fear, worry, and anxiety begins with confronting your fears. Panicking is not normal behavior. It is not healthy to run away from God's call on your life, from people who make you feel uncomfortable, or things that you know in your heart you are supposed to do. It's not good for you to spend your time worrying, thinking about worst-case scenarios and everything that can possibly go wrong. You must take a close look at your life and recognize when fear is controlling you and telling you what you can and cannot do. You've got to admit that you see strongholds of fear, worry, or anxiety operating in your life and declare that you want to be set free. That's the first step in pulling it down.

Step Two: Find the root of your fears, worries, and anxieties

After seeing and admitting that a stronghold of fear, worry, or anxiety is a problem in your life, you next must allow the Lord to take you to where it entered. Whatever your experiences have been, pray and ask God to show you the root of fear in your life. Then, speak that the stronghold of fear, worry, or anxiety is broken off of you and it cannot operate in your life any longer. Refuse to be motivated or moved by fear any longer.

Step Three: Renew your mind to the truth of what God says about fear

The third and final step to pulling down the strongholds of fear, anxiety, and worry is to renew your mind to what God says. His Word tells us the truth about fear. The remaining section of this chapter will show you how to use the Word of God to transform you and break the chains of fear, worry, and anxiety that have had you bound.

Whose battle is it anyway?

Fear will always tell you where you can and can't go and what you can or can't do. Fear chokes you. Fear limits you.

However, you have an Abba Father you can run to any time for help to face your fear. He is your daddy who loves you, not a distant deity unconcerned about your life. God will be responsible for you. Second Chronicles 20:15 NKJV declares, *The Lord says to you, do not be afraid or dismayed because of this multitude, for the battle is not yours, but God's.* The Lord likes you to depend on Him. John 15:5 says, *Apart from Me [that is, cut off from vital union with Me] you can do nothing.* Scripture goes on to say that *all things are possible for the one who believes and trusts [in Me]!* (Mark 9:23)

When you continually worry about a situation, it shows God that you are trying to solve a problem on your own. The Bible says in Proverbs 29:25, *The fear of man brings a snare, But whoever trusts in and puts his confidence in the Lord will be exalted and safe.* Later in this chapter, I'll share the story of how I learned this lesson on one of my missions to Thailand and Myanmar. I had been thinking that the success of the trip was up to me entirely, rather than remembering that it is God who fights my battles. I trusted the Lord and He gave me a supernatural experience. I will always remember that He was there for me no matter how big or small a thing I needed to do. His presence was with me.

Conquering fear...spirt, soul, and body

Franklin Roosevelt once said, "We have nothing to fear but fear itself." Most often, it is fear that is the problem, not the thing we're actually afraid of. How are Christians to deal with fear? Once you've recognized this stronghold in your life and found the root of how it entered your heart, how do you renew your mind to conquer this fear? The answers are in the Word of God and the concept of spirit, soul, and body.

Before we were born again and our spirits made alive, it was difficult for us to take control of our thoughts. Some of us were nervous, depressed—totally controlled by fear, worry, and anxiety. We turned to alcohol or drugs to help us cope. We were predisposed to worry, and we allowed fearful thoughts to run wild in our minds, causing ridiculous imaginations and anxieties.

However, being born again changes everything. Now, we have the Lord to help us. Romans 8:15 expresses it this way: *For you have not received a spirit of slavery leading again to fear [of God's judgment], but you have received the Spirit of adoption as sons [the Spirit producing sonship] by which we [joyfully] cry, "Abba! Father!"*

You can take your fears to your Abba Father now, and with His help, be bold, courageous, and adventurous. I'd like to share some verses to help you renew your mind and replace the lies of your stronghold of fear with the truth of God's Word. Through these Scriptures, we are able to replace lies with truth.

God's Word tells us to take our fear, worry, and anxiety to God. First Peter 5:7 says, *Casting the whole of your care (all your anxieties, all your worries, all your concerns, once and of all) on Him for He cares for you affectionately and cares about you watchfully.*

In addition to 1 Peter 5:7, the Bible states 365 times to *fear not*. We need to take control over fearful and negative thoughts. In Joshua 1:9, we read how the Spirit of God encouraged Joshua, *Have I not commanded you? Be strong, vigorous, and very courageous. Be not afraid for the Lord your God is with you wherever you go.*

When Joshua stepped into leadership upon the death of Moses, he had to choose to walk in the promises he had heard. Joshua used the Holy Spirit's words to take his authority and declare that God would give his people their promised land, saying, *The Lord your God is giving you rest (peace) and will give you this land [east of the Jordan].* (Joshua 1:13) Joshua's example shows that the word coming out of your mouth, or out of your mind, can be the single-most effective weapon against fear, worry, and anxiety. You can stop fears and worries dead in their tracks through your words.

Finally, 2 Corinthians 10:4-5 KJV reminds us of our power in God to overcome strongholds, *(For the weapons of our warfare are not carnal, but mighty through God to the* **pulling down of strong holds;)** **Casting down imaginations, and every high thing that exalteth itself against the knowledge of God**, *and bringing into captivity every thought to the obedience of Christ.*

Go to God

No one can do this for you; you must do it yourself. However, you may still wonder, specifically, how do I do this? The example of King David in Samuel 30:6 is our answer. When the Amalekites invaded and took his people captive, *David was greatly distressed, for all the men spoke of stoning him because the souls of them were bitterly grieved each man for his son and daughter. But, David encouraged and strengthened himself in the Lord his God.*

The last part of this verse is key—David encouraged and strengthened himself in the Lord his God. This is exactly what you should do too when fear, worry, and anxieties seem to take over due to a situation. You must humble yourself and get alone with God. Cry out to Him. You are His child whom He dearly loves and wants to help. In verse 18 of this chapter, we learn that David recovered all that the Amalekites had carried away. God told him what to do. He did it, and his crisis was soon solved.

So, remember, you need to **"take time apart"** or you **"will fall apart**." Time alone with Him and His Word will get you through the problems in life that can give you fear, worry, and anxiety. Paul exhorts believers to understand the importance of spending time with God in Philippians 4:6-7, *Do not be anxious or worried about anything, but in everything [every circumstance and situation] by prayer and petition with thanksgiving, continue to make your [specific] requests known to God. And the peace of God [that peace which reassures the heart, that peace] which transcends all understanding, [that peace which] stands guard over your hearts and your minds in Christ Jesus [is yours].* From these verses, we see that prayer dispels fear!

Renewing your mind: Your authority over fear

Through the previous sections, you see that you need to take your cares to the Lord, remembering that He is always with you and that He'll fight your battles for you. Then you must do your part to remove thoughts of fear from your soul. You need to speak the truth from the Word of God and take authority over the works of the devil—the source of your needless fears. Luke 10:19 declares, *Listen carefully: I have given you authority* [that you now possess] *to tread on serpents and scorpions, and* [the ability to exercise authority] *over all the power of the enemy (Satan); and nothing will* [in any way] *harm you.*

The enemy may have an assignment against you, but you have authority to cancel this assignment. Through your authority, you declare that any negative words spoken over you or any vow that you made in your heart is renounced. Speak that it is over and that you will not allow it to operate in your life any longer. Ultimately, you have a choice to make. You can choose to accept fear or choose to trust God and His Word.

Victory in trust and rest

Every year, I lead mission teams from our Bible college as well as our own ministry to foreign countries. As they anticipate their trip, the students often become loaded with fear, worry, and anxiety. It takes weeks to prepare them and stop their vain imaginations over what they cannot do or the potentially harmful situations that may come their way. However, after their mission trip is over, they see how their fears never came to pass. They learned to trust God. **Trust** is a confident expectation of something and hope and confidence in the ability or intention of a person. The person we trust is Jesus Christ—who is alive!

This trust then leads us to a sense of **peace**. Psalm 37:7 teaches us, *Be still before the Lord; wait patiently for Him and entrust yourself to Him; Do not fret (whine, agonize) because of him who prospers in his way, Because of the man who carries out wicked schemes.*

Rest is the freedom from things that worry, trouble, or disturb. It is a mental or spiritual calm, tranquility, or peace. When fear, worry, and anxiety come knocking at your door—and they do for all of us—**pray, stand on and confess the Word, and choose to trust God**. Psalm 121:1-2 says, I will lift up my eyes to the hills [of Jerusalem]—From where shall my help come? My help comes from the Lord, Who made heaven and earth.

An example of the power of overcoming fear

I want to share with you the following story of how I nearly let fear keep me from one of the most amazing ministry experiences of my life. Remember, our enemy wants to use strongholds to keep us from our destinies—in this story, you'll see how this almost happened to me.

I have served as a short-term missionary for over 40 years, travelling to over 60 countries all over the world. I usually travel with either my husband or a long-time friend and fellow missionary. I am experienced and comfortable with missionary travels and the challenges involved in missionary work. However, a few years ago I faced a new situation in my missionary work that had me in tears and bound with fear.

I had been invited to Thailand and Myanmar for a series of women's conferences and planned to travel with my friend and ministry partner who usually travels with me. At the last minute, my friend's husband got sick, so she canceled her ticket. This meant that I would have to travel to this remote area without a companion. At the thought of this, fear began to grip me.

Right before we were to leave, my friend's husband was healed (praise God!), but unfortunately, the airline told us that it would be extremely difficult, if not impossible, for my friend to repurchase her ticket at the last minute. She was able to be put on a waiting list. I had everyone I know praying for a ticket for her. I could not imagine myself going alone. How could I teach three meetings per day and pray for hundreds of people without someone else? I literally felt sick to my stomach. The more I thought about it, the more panic I let in. I just could not go.

I convinced myself that my husband would agree with my idea to cancel the trip. However, he did not. Finally, the day before we were to leave, my husband said, "Your friend is not going to be able to go with you." I was so upset at him for pointing out the obvious. I went upstairs to my prayer chair to tell the Lord how I just couldn't go alone and would have to cancel the trip. I expected Him to agree with me.

However, the Lord had different ideas. "Oh, so you're going **alone**? What about Me?" I heard Him say. I felt His disappointment in my thinking that I would be alone. I felt His hurt, and I just cried. Fear, anxiety, and worry overwhelmed me because I had forgotten I had the King of kings going with me. I thought about Moses who was so fearful and worried about leading the Israelites to the Promised Land. He made a drama out of his fears just like I was doing. What did the Lord say to Moses with all of his excuses? *My presence shall go with you, and I will give you rest [by bringing you and the people into the promised land].* (Exodus 33:14)

Finally, I decided to go, realizing that God would go with me. What I experienced during those two weeks was absolutely supernatural. I saw God's amazing grace in a brand-new way. I had supernatural confidence, strength, and energy. This trip turned out to be one of my most memorable missionary experiences. God worked through me to bless so many women in those countries, and it almost didn't occur because of a stronghold of fear. What if I had let my fears take over and had canceled the trip? Instead, I tore down those strongholds and saw God's faithfulness and power.

Final thoughts on the stronghold of fear

My experiences in Myanmar and Thailand exposed me to some powerful truths. If we all would remember that the Lord goes with us wherever we go, we could do whatever He calls us to do for Him. We would not let fear strangle us or keep us from living outside of His power. We don't need to be paralyzed or miserable by emotions of fear, worry, and anxiety. We need to renew our minds with the truth that God never leaves us or forsakes us. (Deuteronomy 31:6)

First, I had to realize that I had a stronghold of fear. Next, I had to stamp out the root of rejection, inadequacy, fear of being alone, and lack of trust in the Lord. I had to tear those vain imaginations down and focus on key scriptures. Finally, I had to renew my mind with the truth that God was going with me on the trip.

You may have things in your past that you wish you would have done but didn't. Don't fret over the past, instead make the decision to take your fears to the Lord. You may have things now that you're afraid of doing—don't let the enemy win. You can do all things through Jesus Christ who strengthens you—this scripture in Philippians 4:13 is alive and true for you and your situation. With God's help, you can use the steps given in this chapter and pull down the strongholds of fear, worry, and anxiety.

Self-evaluation questions

- To better understand if you have a stronghold of fear, worry, or anxiety, ask yourself these questions:

- Do I feel a sense of dread or panic in unfamiliar situations, even though this unfamiliar situation is something I know in my mind to be God's will for me?

- Do I feel a sense of dread or panic that determines my course of action?

- Do I find myself constantly worrying about a loved one?

- Do I find myself constantly feeling anxiety over various situations in daily life?

- Do I realize that my fears are irrational, yet succumb to them anyway?

- Has fear seemed to haunt me most of my life?

Scriptures to pull down the stronghold of fear

When fear tries to come against you, here are scriptures you may speak into your life:

For God did not give us a spirit of timidity or cowardice or fear, but [He has given us a spirit] of power and of love and of sound judgment and personal discipline [abilities that result in a calm, well-balanced mind and self-control]. —2 Timothy 1:7

The fear of man brings a snare, But whoever trusts in and puts his confidence in the Lord will be exalted and safe. —Proverbs 20:25

Have I not commanded you? Be strong and courageous! Do not be terrified or dismayed (intimidated), for the Lord your God is with you wherever you go. —Joshua 1:9

Be still before the Lord; wait patiently for Him and entrust yourself to Him; Do not fret (whine, agonize) because of him who prospers in his way, Because of the man who carries out wicked schemes. —Psalm 37:7

The Lord says this to you: "Be not afraid or dismayed at this great multitude, for the battle is not yours, but God's." —2 Chronicles 20:15

For you have not received a spirit of slavery leading again to fear [of God's judgment], but you have received the Spirit of adoption as sons [the Spirit producing sonship] by which we [joyfully] cry, "Abba! Father!" — Romans 8:15

I can do all things [which He has called me to do] through Him who strengthens and empowers me [to fulfill His purpose—I am self-sufficient in Christ's sufficiency; I am ready for anything and equal to anything through Him who infuses me with inner strength and confident peace.] —Philippians 4:13

Casting all your cares [all your anxieties, all your worries, and all your concerns, once and for all] on Him, for He cares about you [with deepest affection, and watches over you very carefully]. —1 Peter 5:7

Chapter Three
Rejection, Low Self-esteem, Guilt, and Shame

I experienced the stronghold of rejection in a traumatic way during my youth. When I was twelve years old, my parents came to me with an important decision they had made. Their decision would strike at the very core of my self-worth. They had decided to send me away to boarding school. I was crushed, feeling that the people whom I needed most to love me and accept me were rejecting me.

Why was that experience so responsible in giving me rejection, low self-esteem, guilt, shame, and other self-imposed negative behaviors? Imagine being with a group of girls who had also been shipped off and made to live together and now had very mean, cold supervisors as their new mothers. We very seldom saw our families. We were totally isolated and had nothing to do but a bunch of strict "do"s and "don't"s. For example, one day, we didn't pass our daily clean room inspection, so at 2:00 AM (right in the middle of the night), we were all awakened and made to take off our mattresses and clean the springs and get the room in top shape. None of my other friends had to go to boarding school. Abandonment, anger, unforgiveness, rebellion, and a host of other emotions followed many of the girls at the boarding school—including me. We all felt trapped with no one to take us out of our misery. This began the story of self-pity and anger that would haunt me for years.

For a long time, that experience affected my life and self-image. It was "my" story that—even after I was saved—I felt I had to continually share. It was my reason and excuse for the rejection, low self-esteem, guilt, and shame I carried around. I was convinced that those feelings would endure throughout my life. Boarding schools were so distressing for the youth that today most have been closed, including the one I was "shipped off" to.

Unfortunately, this stronghold of rejection had repercussions in many areas of my life, causing me to develop many of the other strongholds described in this book. The devil thought he had hit a "homerun" in my life when the spirit of rejection latched onto me. I allowed that experience to define who I was as an unlovable person. It looked as though I would be kept far short of my potential in life. Yet, the Lord would come shining through for me—a Heaven-sent encounter with a stranger would sow the seeds to turn my life around forever. I'll share more about that later in the chapter. It is my hope that through the insights I share, you will be able to recognize the lies that are behind the strongholds of rejection, low self-esteem, guilt, and shame, and be empowered to pull those strongholds down.

Understanding rejection and low self-esteem

Everyone experiences **rejection, low self-esteem, guilt,** and **shame** at some point in his life. While some people are resilient and are able to move on after being rejected, others—particularly people who have gone through repeated rejections—develop a stronghold of rejection. When that happens, they feel rejection, even when no real rejection has occurred. To make matters worse, often low self-esteem and a lack of self-confidence are by-products of the stronghold of rejection.

The definition of rejection is "to refuse to take, accept, or recognize; to throw away or to be treated as useless or unsatisfying." For me, being sent away to boarding school was the ultimate rejection. I became a thoroughly depressed and insecure person. It led to my praying that the Lord would take my life. I could put on the "happy face"; however, inside, my self-image and confidence were terribly low. I asked myself what was wrong with me? The problem was that I believed the lie from Satan that I was not a desirable or lovable person.

Low self-esteem is a feeling that you lack worth. When you look at yourself through the lens of the rejections you perceive or have genuinely experienced (rather than how God sees you), it is easy to fall into low self-esteem.

Rejection...a common problem

No one escapes being hurt at some time or another in life, and the hurts we go through can bring on feelings of rejection and low self-esteem. Even Jesus was rejected; therefore, He totally understands what it is like. The rejection Jesus experienced was accurately prophesied in Isaiah 53:3-4, *He was despised and rejected and forsaken by men, a man of <u>sorrows</u> and <u>pains</u> and acquainted with <u>grief</u> and <u>sickness</u>; and like one from whom people hide their faces, He was <u>despised</u> and we did not appreciate His worth or have any esteem for Him. Surely He has borne our <u>griefs</u> (sicknesses, <u>weaknesses</u>, and <u>distresses</u>) and carried our <u>sorrow</u> and <u>pains</u> (or punishment). Yet we (ignorantly) considered Him stricken, smitten, and afflicted by God (as with leprosy).*

In his life,
  Jesus was betrayed by Judas.
  Jesus was denied by Peter.
  Jesus was forsaken and abandoned by the twelve apostles.

We all—even Jesus—have experienced rejection. Although Jesus experienced hurt and rejection in life, He didn't let it define Him. Unfortunately, most of us let the way we think about ourselves be determined by what has happened to us in the past. Our minds are like a long DVD that consists of what has happened to us from birth until the present. Verbal or sexual abuse, divorce, other experiences that broke our hearts or wounded or disappointed us can continue to control our thoughts.

In your memory bank, you might have stories come up as I did when I asked the Lord to heal my insecurities and low self-esteem and all that made me so void of self-confidence. Maybe some of you were made fun of for the way you looked. Maybe you had acne or you were too thin or too fat. I remember a group of girls in the seventh grade who came up to me and said that I should never wear a dress with my skinny little bird legs. Another time at school, we were told by our gym teacher to play volleyball. Two team captains were picked who were in turn to pick their team members. I was never taught how to play volleyball and wasn't a very good player. I was the last one to be picked and neither of the captains wanted me on her team. Oh, how that hurt. I can laugh now, but for a long time that experience stung my heart.

Maybe you can still remember cruel or demeaning words said to you by your schoolmates, siblings, or parents. Forgive and shake those words off. Don't let their criticism and negative words continue to have power over you and allow you to develop a stronghold of rejection or low self-esteem. Read what the Word says about you. Psalm 139:13 says that you are fearfully and wonderfully made. Jeremiah 1:4-5 says that God knew you before you were formed within your mother's womb. Luke 12:7 says He knows the number of hairs on your head and that you are more valuable than sparrows, not one of which is forgotten by God. Isaiah 45:3-4 says that He knows your name. You must focus on what the Word and the Lord say about you. Let that define you and not the past negative words or things done or said to you.

My story with rejection and low self-esteem

Along with developing depression and insecurity because of the stronghold of rejection, I also became very ill physically. I ended up in the hospital for a month and was told that I had an incurable disease. I felt that my life was over. What I didn't realize was that Jesus Christ was about to give me a brand-new life, free from all the lies and strongholds of my past. Remember in the beginning of the chapter, when I said a Heaven-sent encounter would change my life? Well, the day before I was to leave the hospital, a complete stranger came into my room and told me that Jesus loved me. He also gave me a tract on the book of John. I politely took it, but never thought I would read it. I went home from the hospital and was about to let the devil destroy my destiny. I was just so sick and so sad, I felt that I had nothing left to live for. So, I made plans to end my own life.

The night I planned to commit suicide, I was straightening up a stack of papers when out fell the Christian tract. I somehow felt compelled to read it. For the first time in my life, I was reading the truth from the Bible. As I read John

3:16 KJV, *For God so loved the world that he gave his one and only Son, that whoever believes in him shall not perish but have eternal life*, and John 3:3 NIV, *I tell you the truth, no one can see the kingdom of God unless he is born again*, I was thrilled! Why hadn't I been told this before? I realized that I had a religion—a **knowledge about** God, but I needed a relationship in which I would **know** Him. The next thing I knew, I was on my knees reciting the sinner's prayer written in the tract. All of the suicidal thoughts left. The next morning, I knew something had happened. I felt like a butterfly that had just come out of its ugly cocoon and was ready to fly. That night, I became a "new creature" in Christ. Did all the strongholds drop off immediately? No. But, eventually it did happen—including the painful stronghold of rejection.

Step One: Face the lies

I've already talked about how the first step in pulling down any stronghold is to admit your problem. You cannot break the chains and strongholds that bind you until you face or ask the Lord what you need to work on. What do you overreact to? What upsets or depresses you? Considering these things will help you to recognize a stronghold.

Do you continually speak fearful, negative, angry words? Do you indulge in gossip and lies? Remember, the sad truth about facing and acknowledging strongholds is that often everyone can see them in you, except you yourself. That all comes from your pride—the tunnel vision that comes from self-centeredness. You don't want to admit you have a problem—but you will never move forward until you do.

In a previous chapter, I shared that my husband pointed out my spirit of rejection. He noticed how I would get my feelings hurt and think I was being rejected, when the truth was that the people I was interacting with were just busy. I was overreacting because of the rejection in my heart. Out of the abundance of my heart, I spoke bitterness and rejection. With my husband's help, I came to face the fact that I had a stronghold of rejection. You, too, must acknowledge that stronghold if you're going to defeat it.

Step Two: Find the root of your rejection

After facing the stronghold of rejection, you have to do what it takes to remove it. You cannot get freedom unless you ask God to trace the stronghold back to its its root. You must ask God to show you where the strongholds and vain imaginations started in your life.

The Lord showed me that my stronghold of rejection started when my parents sent me away to boarding school. Often, it is just one incident or trauma that you hang on to, and then it only gets worse. Ask the Lord to help you uncover any incident which caused you to plant rejection in your heart. Perhaps this led to feelings of low self-esteem—that nobody could ever love you, that your life just didn't carry much worth. Let the Lord show you how these types of feelings entered your heart.

Only as you are "rooted" in Him can you "uproot" these negative feelings or actions. Everyone wants to hide insecurities and other negative thoughts, so he wears a "mask" to cover up his real person. Unless you take a good, hard look at yourself, you will never change. Remember, you hold the key to changing!

Step Three: Goodbye rejection!

As I've said previously on the steps to move on and get over your past, you need to stop blaming others and "shake off" what they did to you. My story—that I didn't realize everyone else also has—was finally over when I made the decision to stop making excuses, and to no longer accept that rejection was "my story" and that this was just who I was.

Someone once told me three little words that helped set me free from my past: "Get over it!" This may sound very simple, but it's true. Once you've admitted your stronghold and faced the past, at a certain point, you just need to decide in your heart to give all your hurts to the Lord and get over it.

For me, I had to realize that I had to stop thinking and talking about my past boarding school story. Everyone has something that happened to him that could crush him. Everyone has a "story." The question is: Are you going to let this story dominate the narrative of your life? For many years, I let my traumatic boarding school experience determine my self-worth, rather than realizing my true self-worth and image come from Christ and what He says about me. When I finally did realize this, I had to forgive my parents and move on from my past.

The Bible commands us to let the past stay in the past. Isaiah 43:18 says, *Do not (earnestly) remember the former things; neither consider the things of old.* I had to let go of the unforgiveness, bitterness, and resentment I had towards my parents. When I stopped talking about it, then I stopped thinking about it, and I was on my way to freedom.

As I've explained, low self-esteem can be a result of rejection or negative things done or said to you. Proverbs 23:7 says that as a person thinks in his heart, so he is or will become. In other words, whatever you believe about yourself on the inside is what you will act like or manifest on the outside. Lack of self-confidence can control your life and keep you from being all you were created to be in Christ.

If I hadn't moved forward, I wouldn't be the mentor, minister, teacher, and missionary I am today. You cannot get beyond your own opinion of yourself. Ask God to give you a new self-worth and image. Speak death to and cancel the negative words spoken to or about you. Satan is the "accuser of the brethren." Refuse his accusations. God wants to do a "makeover" on you like He did for these:

    Moses was a stutterer and had no confidence but ended up leading the Israelites to the Promised Land.

    Paul went from hating and persecuting Christians to being a great evangelist for the Lord.

    Peter denied Jesus and was too scared to say He knew Him. He ended up establishing the first church of 3,000 people. Later he was crucified for his faith in Him.

    Mary Magdalene had seven demons cast out of her but went on to follow and help Jesus and was chosen to be the one to announce His resurrection.

Guilt and shame

The last two strongholds in this chapter are guilt and shame. Many amazing people in the Bible once struggled with guilt and shame. Consider the guilt on Paul who once persecuted Christians, and the shame on Mary Magdalene who lived in defilement. Everyone makes mistakes and bad choices, but the Word says in Romans 8:1, *(there is) now no condemnation (no adjudging guilty of wrong) for those who are in Christ Jesus.*

So, what are guilt and shame? Guilt is defined as "feelings of deserving blame especially for imagined offenses or from a sense of inadequacy." When you focus on these negative feelings, you can then develop a sense of shame in which you are overly conscious of guilt and then you develop low self-esteem. Now, there is actually a good kind of guilt called conviction, but Satan gives you something different—his kind of guilt and shame are called condemnation. The most dangerous people are those who walk around with hardened hearts and no guilt, shame, or conviction at all. So, be glad that your heart isn't so hard that you don't even experience these emotions at all—but still you must be ready to move past them.

Pulling down guilt and shame

How do you get rid of guilt and shame? You need to confess your sin—deal with what you did. Admit your mistakes, how you've hurt others and made poor choices. Then, accept His forgiveness as Paul, Mary Magdalene, and others did. First Peter 2:24 reminds us that Jesus has taken all of our sins, *He personally carried our sins in His body on the cross [willingly offering Himself on it, as on an altar of sacrifice], so that we might die to sin [becoming immune from the penalty and power of sin] and live for righteousness; for by His wounds you [who believe] have been healed.* Also, Isaiah 53:5 confirms this, *But He was wounded for our transgressions, He was crushed for our wickedness [our sin, our injustice, our wrongdoing]; The punishment [required] for our well-being fell on Him, And by His stripes (wounds) we are healed.* Believe and accept that Jesus bore your sins and the consequent guilt, shame, and pain that goes with it. Let God use your mistakes so you can turn around and help others.

I am now a chaplain for the women in jail at Colorado Springs. When I first started, the devil would flood me with thoughts of, "How can you go to minister at the jail when you did things that could have put you in jail, you hypocrite? Don't you remember when…?" At first I started receiving those thoughts, thinking back over some of the past mistakes I'd made, but then I replaced those false accusations with the words and scriptures that you'll find at the end of this chapter. Accept what He did for you. What unconditional love He has for His children. Why should you not be forgiven? Why should you not forgive yourself? Throw off the guilt and shame if your Savior has already done it for you. Isaiah 43:18 says, *Do not remember the former things, neither consider the things of old*. Renew your mind with this verse and be free of guilt and shame.

Avoiding guilt and shame by focusing on God

One final piece of advice in removing guilt and shame from your life: Don't fall into the trap of trying to please people. Being a people-pleaser can result in your having unmerited guilt and shame. Some people spend their lives not doing what they're called to do, but what they think their parents want them to do, feeling guilt about the idea of disappointing their parents. Other people are so concerned about what their peers think of them, that they do things they know are wrong just to fit in—then the guilt and shame come. Being a people-pleaser is a slippery slope. You've got to learn to say "no" to people. Don't be a people-pleaser; rather, be a God-pleaser, and avoid developing strongholds of guilt and shame.

Final thoughts on the stronghold of rejection, low self-esteem, guilt, and shame

We all have to deal with rejection, low self-esteem, guilt, and shame. But we don't have to let our negative experiences replay again and again and limit our futures. We don't have to let either the hurts that have been put on us, nor the hurts we have put on others define us. We can forgive and be forgiven. We can take all our rejection and shame and guilt to Jesus and become the new creation God intends for us to be.

Self-evaluation questions

- To better understand if you have a stronghold of rejection, low self-esteem, guilt, or shame, ask yourself these questions:

- Do I still think about painful, emotional experiences from years ago, when someone didn't choose me?

- Do I have experiences from years past that I've let become "my story" that I feel I must repeatedly share with others?

- Do I overreact to various situations, such as thinking the worst when I don't immediately hear back from someone I have called?

- Do I have lingering feelings of guilt or shame over a mistake I've made in the past?

- Am I a people-pleaser? Do I constantly worry about what people think of me?

- Do my loved ones notice that I often feel rejection, low self-esteem, guilt, or shame without reason?

Scriptures to pull down the strongholds of rejections, low self-esteem, guilt, and shame

When you're attacked with rejection, low self-esteem, guilt, and shame, renew your mind with these scriptures:

He personally carried our sins *in His body on the cross [willingly offering Himself on it, as on an altar of sacrifice], so that we might die to sin [becoming immune from the penalty and power of sin] and live for righteousness; for by His wounds you [who believe] have been healed.* —I Peter 2:24

But He was wounded for our transgressions, He was crushed for our wickedness [our sin, our injustice, our wrongdoing]; The punishment [required] for our well-being fell on Him, And by His stripes (wounds) we are healed. —Isaiah 53:5

There is now no condemnation for those who are in Christ Jesus. —Romans 8:1 NIV

Do not remember the former things, Or ponder the things of the past. —Isaiah 43:18

He heals the brokenhearted And binds up their wounds [healing their pain and comforting their sorrow]. —Psalm 147:3

The *Lord* is near to the heartbroken And He saves those who are crushed in spirit (contrite in heart, truly sorry for their sin). —Psalm 34:18

Chapter Four
Jealousy

Many years ago, my extended family owned a beautiful house on a breathtaking lake. This property had been in the family for many years. My children, husband, and I spent many delightful weekends there, swimming, skiing, and sailing. The setting was idyllic and the memories we made there were precious. We expected to be able to continue to enjoy the use of the property for many years to come. Yet, one day, it all ended. I got a call from a friend informing me that at the end of the summer season, the house had been torn down and a huge, gorgeous new house was being built there in its place. "How could this be?" I wondered. The lake house was an important part of my life, and I had not been included at all in the decision to develop a new house on the property.

I called the family member who was in charge of the property to find out if my friend's report was true. He confirmed everything and told me that we would no longer have access to the new house and would just have to find another place or buy our own house. When I asked if we could still visit, the answer was, "No." I was crushed. Weren't we family? What would my parents say if they were still alive? The lake house was for all of us to enjoy. My anger at this injustice began to build. I was so upset that important decisions had been made behind my back and that I was told that we could not even visit the property—it felt like a harsh slap in the face. I did want to get over it, but so many strongholds were strangling me that I couldn't move on.

However, the Lord knows we are human, and that other people will betray and let us down. I realized that I had fallen into a trap from Satan by not being able to forgive my relatives. My husband told me that I had no choice and that I had to be careful because I was setting the example for my children, who were watching me. Plus, my negative feelings went against everything the Bible said about jealousy and unforgiveness. Finally, one day,

I decided to deal with it—a stronghold of jealousy was starting to develop that I knew I didn't want. I needed to move on, but first, I had to confront the jealousy in my heart. I'll show you how I did so through this chapter.

Jealousy…a warning from God

The Bible is a book, not only of promises and blessings from the Lord, but also of warnings and guidelines. One of these warnings is to guard ourselves from jealousy. Consider this warning in 2 Timothy 3:1-2, *But understand this, that in the last days dangerous times [of great stress and trouble] will come [difficult days that will be hard to bear]. For people will be lovers of self [narcissistic, self-focused], lovers of money [impelled by greed], boastful, arrogant, revilers, disobedient to parents, ungrateful, unholy and profane.*

Problems with jealousy are not just in these last days but may be seen in the Bible from the beginning. Exodus 20:17 commands, *You shall not covet your neighbor's house, your neighbor's wife or his manservants, or his ox, or his donkey, or anything that is your neighbor's.* Through these verses, God has given us explicit directions on not allowing jealousy into our hearts.

A story of Cain and Abel in Genesis 4:1-8 illustrates the problem and tragic results of jealousy. Cain brought fruit as an offering to the Lord, but Abel brought the first of his flocks, a much more meaningful sacrifice. Cain offered the least, while his brother offered the best. The Bible says God had no respect for Cain and his offering, but instead respected Abel and his offering. Cain felt angry and dejected. Cain's anger and jealousy grew to the point that he killed his own brother, Abel. We would never use a physical weapon to harm someone, but we must consider that sometimes we slay people with the word of our tongues.

Jealousy is not just in the Bible. I have heard countless stories in which jealousy that was not dealt with led to terrible consequences. One tragic example that I know of involves a woman who discovered that her husband was having an affair. Despite this painful offense, she still had many positives in her life, including her children and her successful career as a dentist.

Her husband later promised to stop seeing the other woman. However, one night he went out, and the suspicious wife secretly followed him to a hotel. She waited and waited, and her husband eventually walked out with the other woman. Overcome with jealousy, she drove her car over him and killed him. Tragically, this woman had just had twin babies that she will never be able to raise because she is serving a life sentence in prison. Had she taken control of the jealousy instead of letting it control her, today she would still be a dentist and would have the joy of raising her children.

Jealousy: The root of other griefs

When I did a word study on jealousy, I found it interesting how many other negative words are associated with this one word. Jealousy is "the feeling of envy, resentment, suspicious fear, greed, covetousness (an extreme desire for something; to desire wrongfully for what is not yours); discontent (usually at seeing another's superiority, advantage, possessions, attainment); unhappiness because of someone else's possessions, achievements, or blessings; begrudging." Jealousy clearly gives birth to a host of destructive feelings in our lives.

Sadly, the world is full of these negative feelings; unfortunately, Christians are too. Because of our flesh, it is normal to be tempted to have jealousy, but we must not allow it to control our thoughts or actions toward others since we are not to be led by the flesh, but by the Spirit. Rather, we should look at others and ourselves through the filter of God's love for us all.

Additional warnings on jealousy

Society tells us that happiness and contentment come from wealth, success, and possessions. The truth is that these can never satisfy us. Ecclesiastes 5:10 speaks to this fact: *He who loves money will not be satisfied with money, nor he who loves abundance with its gain. This too is vanity (emptiness).*

The Bible gives us yet another warning on jealousy in Luke 12:15, *Then He said to them, "Watch out and guard yourselves against every form of greed; for not even when one has an overflowing abundance does his life consist of nor is it derived from his possessions."* Clearly, we have been given ample warning to avoid looking to find happiness in material wealth.

We need to resist jealousy because it can destroy relationships—marriages, friendships, and other important bonds. Remember the example of the woman who was jealous over her husband's affair? Sadly, this jealousy caused her to act in a way that damaged her relationship with her precious babies.

Jealousy can destroy or hurt any type of ministry or our witness to others. The devil uses jealousy to keep Christians from working together. When I lead mission trips, he many times tries to stir up strife and disharmony by throwing in jealousy. Rather than focusing on evangelizing and ministering to unsaved people, sometimes the mission teams focus on their negative, jealous feelings toward their fellow Christians.

Not only will we have to fight feelings of jealousy toward other people's material possessions, there will also be plenty of opportunities for jealousy to come knocking at our door in other areas of our lives. For example, when we hear about someone else's success or a promotion of a coworker for a new job that we wanted, or when we see people that seem to have a perfect family and perfect marriage, we may be tempted with feelings of jealousy. Look at the story of King Saul and David found in 1 Samuel. David only wanted to bless Saul but ended up being more popular and a better warrior than Saul. The king couldn't handle that David was getting more attention, so he sought to kill him. Romans 12:15 says, *Rejoice with those who rejoice (sharing other's joy), and weep with those who weep (sharing other's grief).*

We also need to be aware of tendencies toward being jealous over the talent we see in others. Some talents just tend to naturally receive more attention. But we have to remember that God made each of us unique with special gifts that are important regardless of the attention we receive for them. If you're not sure what your talents are, ask God to show you—we are all fearfully and wonderfully made. (Psalm 139:14) Being jealous over the gifts of others can result in damaged relationships and not being able to work together with them the way that God intended.

In addition, people will be jealous of us—yes, our Christian friends will give in to feelings of jealousy. My husband and I were blessed with a beautiful house from the Lord. We got an amazing price on the house, and we know it was the Lord who got us the deal. Some friends were very happy for us; others challenged us with jealous comments such as, "You must have won the lottery to get a house like this."

On another occasion, I received a seven-page letter from a lady who I thought was a friend. This letter was full of lies and false accusations; yet, she signed it, "Praying for you." When I asked the Lord why she did this even though I had been a good friend to her, He said one word: "Jealousy!"

If friends turn on you, gossip about you, falsely accuse you, and betray you, it is likely because of jealousy. The Bible is filled with stories of jealousy, including stories like Joseph and his brothers as well as the stories of Cain and Abel and David and King Saul. In addition, the Pharisees were also terribly jealous of Jesus. All these stories are examples that can guide you in what to do when jealousy arises. The people in the Bible who overcame jealousy both forgave and forgot and went on. (Forgiveness is an important topic, and I'll devote a whole chapter to later.)

You will never be happy or satisfied if you let thoughts of jealousy control your life. Yet another warning on jealousy is in James 3:16, *For wherever there is jealousy (envy) and contention (rivalry and selfish ambition), there will also be confusion (unrest, disharmony, rebellion) and all sorts of evil and vile practice.*

Step One: Pulling down jealousy

Jealousy is destructive and clearly must be pulled down. As with any stronghold, the first step is to acknowledge the problem. To overcome jealousy, you must confront this negative emotion and admit that you struggle with thoughts of jealousy. Remember that you cannot conquer what you will not confront!

You need to deeply consider how you view wealth and possessions. It is a tool of the enemy to have you work and struggle for material possessions and success when the truth is that none of your material possessions will go with you when you die. Only what you give or do for the Lord will last forever in eternity and can be taken with you to heaven where you will be rewarded. That is something to think about. I have been at many wealthy people's funerals—all their material possessions separated from them forever when they died.

You must also consider whether you are jealous in other aspects of life as well, such as jealousy over physical appearance, natural talents, relationships, and more. Jealousy in any area of life is harmful and must be confronted.

Step Two: Find the root

If jealousy isn't dealt with, it can lead to a spirit or stronghold that controls you. The root cause of jealousy is often insecurity. When you are confident and secure in who you are and how God loves you and sees you, then your heart will be protected from jealousy. Putting your trust in anything other than God can lead to feelings of insecurity.

Ask God to show you if you have any insecurity that needs to be dealt with and ask Him to show you how this insecurity entered your life. You might have suffered an injustice but never dealt with your feelings. Perhaps, as a child, you perceived that others around you were better loved and thus became jealous. Allow God to show you when you first began to struggle with feelings of jealousy.

Step Three: Renew your mind

You need to ask the Lord to renew your mind so that jealousy will not operate in your life. The choice is up to you to resist or entertain jealousy. You need to strive to be content instead of focusing on what others have that you wish you had. Hebrews 13:5 confirms this: *Let your character [your moral essence, your inner nature] be free from the love of money [shun greed—be financially ethical], being content with what you have; for He has said, "I will never [under any circumstances] desert you [nor give you up nor leave you without support, nor will I in any degree leave you helpless], nor will I forsake or let you down or relax My hold on you [assuredly not]!"* These words are spoken to you—God will never leave you nor forsake you. There could be no greater reason to ever feel insecure again. Ask God to make you a secure person so that when others are blessed with promotions or materials things, you are okay with it.

Remember the story about the beautiful lake house from the beginning of the chapter? To move on from this let-down in my life, I had to confront jealousy and get closure on my disappointment. I knew I had to see the finished house and ask God to help me accept the changes that had occurred. I knew I couldn't do it myself, but I gave the Lord permission to change my heart. As I drove up the road and was going around the curve where I saw the gorgeous property which I no longer had any claim to, the Lord spoke to my heart and told me, "Peggy, you are only passing by, let it go. Life is but a vapor."

I then realized how carnal I was being. I am on the earth just a short time, yet I was letting what happened over the house ruin my life. Someday, I will be gone and who knows what will become of the house in time. I understood in my heart the truth of the situation and was set free! Later, I remembered how James 4:14 tells us, *Yet you do not know [the least thing] about what may happen in your life tomorrow. [What is secure in your life?] You are merely a vapor [like a puff of smoke or a wisp of steam from a cooking pot] that is visible for a little while and then vanishes [into thin air]*. That thought gave me a completely different perspective.

The Value of a Grateful Heart

One more thing to help you pull down the stronghold of jealousy, is to take time to remember all the things you do have instead of focusing on what you don't have. Stop comparing yourselves with others and their talents, appearance, houses, jobs, cars, and various possessions. When I travel as a missionary around the world, I find that people in other nations who watch American movies or television think all Americans are all millionaires and have cars and houses like the ones shown on the screen. We all know that this is not true. However, if you were to go to most countries around the world and see how they live, you would be so thankful for what you have. But remember that God does like to bless us. We know this is true from Psalm 35:27 which tells us that God takes pleasure in the prosperity of His children. The key is to be aware and thankful for God's blessings in your life.

Related to thankfulness is contentment. Contentment is having your desires limited to what you have, not want; to be satisfied and to not complain about what you do not have. Contentment brings satisfaction, enjoyment, and pleasure—exactly the opposite of what jealousy brings. Being content will be a learning process for some of you. This was true for Paul, who explains in Philippians 4:11, *I have learned to be content [and self-sufficient through Christ, satisfied to the point where I am not disturbed or uneasy] regardless of my circumstances.*

The key to contentment is to realize that God has given you everything you need to remain victorious in Christ. Only Christ (and being in Him) can truly satisfy all your needs.

Self-evaluation questions

To understand if you have a stronghold of jealousy, ask yourself these questions:

- Do I feel envy over others' good fortunes? Do I wish I had a better car, a better house, better clothes, etc.?

- Do I find that the relationships in my life suffer because of feelings of resentment and envy?

- Do I look at other people's relationships and feel upset that life is not fair?

- Do I wish I had different gifts and talents, like the ones I see in others?

- Have there been times when I let jealousy stop me from working with other Christians as God intended? Has it stopped me from doing the ministry I know I am called to?

- Do I spend time thanking God for the blessings in my life?

- Am I content with what I have, or do I always want more?

Scriptures to pull down the stronghold of jealousy

When jealousy tries to surface in your life, speak and do these scriptures:

Not that I speak from [any personal] need, for I have learned to be content [and self-sufficient through Christ, satisfied to the point where I am not disturbed or uneasy] regardless of my circumstances. —Philippians 4:11

Let them shout for joy and rejoice, who favor my vindication and want what is right for me; Let them say continually, "Let the Lord be magnified, who delights and takes pleasure in the prosperity of His servant." —Psalm 35:27

Let your conversation be without covetousness and be content with such things as you have; for he hath said, I will never leave thee nor forsake thee. —Hebrews 13:5 KJV

Let the peace of Christ rule in your hearts, since as members of one body you were called to peace. And be thankful. —Colossians 3:15 NIV

Rooted and built up in him, strengthened in the faith as you were taught, and overflowing with thankfulness. —Colossians 2:7 NIV

Therefore, since we are receiving a kingdom that cannot be shaken, let us be thankful, and so worship God acceptably with reverence and awe. —Hebrews 12:28 NIV

The LORD *is my strength and my shield; my heart trusts in him, and he helps me. My heart leaps for joy, and with my song I praise him.* — Psalm 28:7 NIV

I will give thanks and praise the Lord, with all my heart; I will tell aloud all Your wonders and marvelous deeds. —Psalm 9:1

Chapter Five
Offense and Bitterness

My husband and I served as associate pastors in a large ministry many years ago. One night, I received a phone call from one of our lead elders. She told me she had heard about a dramatic situation that was supposedly happening in my marriage. She went on to say, "But don't worry; I've put the problem on the church's prayer chain." Well, it was a total "soap opera" lie which I discovered was being circulated by another minister and his wife. I was devastated! Why were these Christian ministers spreading this lie about us?

I was young in the ministry and totally offended. I proceeded to tell my husband that I was quitting the ministry. I told him to take the children to church for the next service, but I would not be returning. After they left, I sat down to talk to the Lord about the situation—totally expecting Him to comfort me and confirm my decision to quit. He is our Father and will speak to us if we just ask. When I poured out my heart to Him and reminded Him of what He said in Isaiah 54:17 that *No weapon that is formed against me will succeed*, He promptly replied that I was the one letting this whole thing prosper through my reaction of unforgiveness, anger, and the decision to quit the ministry. He told me that the devil was using this couple and their own problems and jealousy towards my husband and me in an attempt to destroy our reputation. It was his trap, and I had fallen into it.

When God told me all this, it was such a revelation to me. This whole plan to get me to quit and be full of unforgiveness was Satan's doing. Next, He told me to forgive them. I told Him back, "But these are not only Christians, but ministers. I just can't." He answered by saying, "My Word doesn't <u>ask</u> you to forgive but <u>tells</u> you to release them to me." I told Him again that <u>I</u> couldn't, to which He said that my selfish *phileo* love couldn't but, if I put on the nature of Christ and used His *agape* love toward these people, I could.

My pride and stubbornness were raging, but I knew I had to be obedient—so I was. That Sunday night, I went back to church and forgave my offenders, stopping the stronghold of offense from growing. I never heard another word about the lie. I chose to let it go. Later, the couple divorced and were removed from their positions. God had totally vindicated us which is the promise at the end of Isaiah 54:17, *"No weapon that is formed against you will succeed; And every tongue that rises against you in judgment you will condemn. This [peace, righteousness, security, and triumph over opposition] is the heritage of the servants of the Lord, And this is their vindication from Me," says the Lord.*

Understanding offense

It is impossible for you to not be offended by someone in this life. The Bible supports this in Luke 17:1 KJV, *It is impossible but that offenses will come; but woe unto him through whom they come.*

We must realize that Satan hides behind every offense. He uses people to carry out his plans to trap us in an offense and bring on unforgiveness, bitterness, and other strongholds. I see this happening before mission trips or ministry meetings. The Lord warned me that these problems are sent from Satan to distract me from preparing and being totally involved in my meetings. We need to be prudent and wise enough to not fall into the devil's plan. Luke 17:1 records Jesus telling His disciples, *Temptations (snares, traps set to entice sin) are sure to come.*

The Greek word for offense is *skandalon*. It means "laying a trap in someone's way." Having an offense come your way is not the problem. The problem comes when you fall into Satan's trap by picking up the offense, dwelling on it, and letting it reside in your heart. You must be prepared and be armed because your response to an offense will determine your success in your journey of life. What happens when you get hurt or offended? If you don't get rid of an offense right away, it can lead to negative emotions such as anger, depression, rejection, resentment, strife, hatred, bitterness, and many more. Often, people hide behind "masks" to cover up what is bothering them. This denial and refusal to deal with an offense is just what Satan wants.

The devil also wants you to feel that you are the only one to whom a negative thing has happened. After years of ministry and counseling, I can tell you that "your story" is very similar to what has happened to hundreds of other people. The facts may not be identical but, around the world, the devil dishes out the same problems to destroy every person he can. First Peter 5:8 says that Satan goes *around as a roaring lion seeking whom he may devour.* In a sense, he stalks you, and because of this, you need to know your authority over him and his plans. This is why you need to watch out for the "victim mentality" which causes you to feel entitled to hang on to past problems.

This is also why the Bible says—rather commands—to let the past stay in the past.
Consider Philippians 3:13 which says, *I do not consider, brethren, that I have captured and made it my own (yet); but one thing I do (it is my one aspiration): forgetting what lies behind and straining forward to what lies ahead.* Isaiah 43:18 also warns us to let go of the past. It says, *Do not (earnestly) remember the former things; neither consider the things of old.*

When I was first saved, I truly had a radical conversion, but I didn't know these scriptures. I would go around sharing my story of being sent away to boarding school, keeping the chains of rejection and other strongholds wrapped around me. For some of you, "your story" is a way to get attention or have people feel sorry for you. It can help you feel entitled to hold on to your chains.

If you do not forgive, let go, and try to get over what happened to you, you develop strongholds or vain imaginations. Proverbs 23:7 confirms that this is true, *As you think in your heart, so you are and will act.*

I had to forgive my parents for sending me away to boarding school. So, one day I wrote them a letter telling them that I forgave them. I wanted them to be the ones to apologize, but I knew it would never happen. They weren't saved and didn't see the problems their decisions caused in my life. Many of you won't forgive because it was the other person's fault and you are waiting for an apology that will never happen. No matter whose fault it was, just step out in faith, put on the nature of Christ, and forgive them anyway.

We started this section with Luke 17:1 telling us that there is no way you are going to escape being offended. The second part of the scripture says, B*ut woe unto him through whom they come!* God will deal with the people who hurt you. A person will reap what he has sown. Our business is to give these people to Him and let God deal with them. We all are going to die one day, and over and over the Word tells us we will all be accountable for what we have done in this life and will be judged accordingly.

Remember, you must see life with this mindset: your <u>past</u> is over. You can't change it. Your <u>present</u> is a gift from God. Enjoy it. Your <u>future</u> is a mystery. Look forward to it with expectation.

The closer the relationship, the deeper the offense

It is one thing to get hurt by someone who is not saved, but another thing to get hurt by another brother or sister in Christ. You are not the only one who has suffered in this way. For example, King David was hurt by a close friend and explained his feelings in Psalm 55:12-14: For it is not an enemy who taunts me—Then I could bear it; Nor is it one who has hated me who insolently exalts himself against me—Then I could hide from him. But it is you, a man my equal and my counsel, My companion and my familiar friend; We who had sweet fellowship together, Who walked to the house of God in company.

Remember, the <u>greater the expectation</u> of someone, the <u>greater the hurt</u>. I experienced this but picked myself back up and went on after the offense that happened through the fellow ministers at my church. This wasn't the last hurt I have had from Christians, but after almost forty years of ministry, I have learned who the real person behind all this is. He is defeated and under my feet, and so I throw his hurt back at him and through Christ, I forgive and "shake it off."

It is a fact that the closer the relationship, the more severe the offense. For example, the people you look up to or trust as a family member or close friend could easily hurt you and disappoint you. The old expression, "you only hurt the ones you love" is so true. If someone you don't know or care about betrays you, it is easier to get over than when someone you trusted and welcomed into your life betrays you. The offender was your friend or family member whom you thought you could count on. This kind of hurt can break our hearts. Proverbs 18:14 describes a wounded spirit: *The spirit of a man sustains him in sickness, But as for a broken spirit, who can bear it?*

Here is a story from William Barclay that shows the tragedy of a broken heart: "A man can stand almost any attack on his body, the thing that beats him is a broken heart. It is told that in the days of Hitler, there was a man in Germany who was arrested, tried, tortured, and put into a concentration camp. He faced it with all gallantry and emerged erect and unbroken. Then, by accident, he discovered who it was who had laid information against him. It was his own son. The discovery broke his heart and he died. An attack by an enemy he could bear; but this attack from someone he loved is what killed him."

Thank God, the Word says in Psalm 147:3, *He heals the brokenhearted And binds up their wounds [healing their pain and comforting their sorrow]*.

Offense toward God...the seeds of bitterness

In addition to being offended at people, it is also possible to be offended at God. Everyone has had prayers that were not answered the way they wanted them to be. For example, you may have prayed for people who were not healed, or you may have prayed for jobs and many other things that didn't come to pass even after you prayed and believed. The devil loves when this happens, and he takes full advantage to steal your faith and trust in God. The Bible reminds us that God is above our understanding—Isaiah 55:9 says that His ways are not our ways; they are higher. We cannot let our lack of understanding undermine our faith in God. In Matthew 24:10, the Bible also warns us to not take offense toward God, *At that time many will be offended and repelled [by their association with Me] and will fall away [from the One whom they should trust] and will betray one another [handing over believers to their persecutors] and will hate one another.*

Take no offense...flow in blessings

Let's look at two examples from the Bible of men who refused to become offended at God as well as at man.

The first story is about Joseph. It is found in Genesis Chapters 37-50. After reading these chapters, you can understand how Joseph had a list of reasons why he would not want to forgive the many people who betrayed him, including his own brothers who sold him into slavery. He could have questioned God as to why He let it all happen. But, because of his forgiving attitude and refusal to hold on to offenses, the Lord was with Joseph and promoted him from a prisoner to the prime minister!

David is another example of someone who was mistreated but refused Satan's trap of offense and took no revenge. His story is found in 1 Samuel 16-31. From reading these chapters, you can see that David loved Saul and, as I mentioned in a previous chapter, served him faithfully. King Saul, like Joseph's brothers in the story above, was jealous of David and tried to kill him. David could have killed him, but he chose not to take revenge. Because of David's willingness to forgive, he went from being a shepherd boy to a king!

Absolutely no man, woman, child, or demon can get you out of the will and plan of God for your life unless you allow them to. When you forgive, rather than smoldering in offense, you allow blessings to flow into your life. What are you holding back through the unforgiveness in your heart?

Step One: Face the offense and unforgiveness in your heart

So, how do you get free from offense, unforgiveness, and possible bitterness? Why is it so hard to do? Often, your own stubborn pride gets in the way. Your ego makes you pretend that you are controlling those who hurt you by punishing them. You are trying to manipulate others through unforgiveness. You try to do justice on your own terms—but, in reality, you do yourself an injustice by creating a situation in which your heart lets in bitterness.

So where do we begin? You first need to acknowledge the people who have offended you that you can't seem to forgive or get free from. Talk to the Lord or another person about the hurt or offense that is still bothering you. You need to get it out!

Step Two: Get to the root

To pull down this stronghold, you've got to go to the root of when the offense first took place. Forgive the offense at the very point at which it first occurred. Ask the Lord to show you the root of your offense and unforgiveness. Often, many subsequent offenses take place after an initial hurt, and these all need to be forgiven as well, but the key is to go back to the origin of the hurt and be willing to forgive from the very point at which you were offended.

Gain freedom through forgiveness

Before moving on to the third step, we need to take a close look at forgiveness—you won't be able to move forward in pulling down this stronghold until you truly forgive.

The Parable of the Unmerciful Servant (Matthew 18:21-35) shows us that we need to be generous in our forgiving: *My heavenly Father will also do the same to [every one of] you, if each of you does not forgive his brother from your heart.* (verse 35) Forgive as an act of your will, not because the person you are forgiving deserves it. Forgiveness is a gift to others and also to yourself, eliminating the poison of unforgiveness. You cannot forgive in your own *phileo* selfish love, but by God's *agape* love that is in you. Choose to put on the nature of Christ. Life becomes easier when you learn to accept an apology you never got. *Above all, have fervent and unfailing love for one another, because love covers a multitude of sins [it overlooks unkindness and unselfishly seeks the best for others].* (1 Peter 4:8)

Swallow your pride and decide to let go of the offense. I once prayed for a woman who had a pain in her shoulder which kept her from raising her arm. When I began to pray for her, I saw in the spirit a big sign over her that said "unforgiveness." When I asked her if she had any issues with unforgiveness, she began to tell me of her husband's adultery which had happened fifteen years earlier but she had never forgiven. Then I asked her if she was ready to forgive and release—she said "yes"—and she was instantly healed! Like this woman, you need to leave people, hurts, and offenses at the feet of Jesus. You need to forgive from your heart. When Jesus was being nailed to the cross, He said, "Father, forgive them for they do not know what they are doing." It is important to note that the people whom Jesus forgave didn't have to apologize first to Jesus in order to receive forgiveness from Him. We, too, can forgive without ever hearing an apology.

The story above exemplifies why it is good for us to forgive. When we forgive, it brings us health and restoration. It cuts the chains that bind us to the people that hurt us. Did you know that, in medical books, unforgiveness is classified as a disease? According to Dr. Standiford, chief of surgery at the Cancer Treatment Centers of America, refusing to forgive others makes people sick and keeps them in illness. With that in mind, forgiveness therapy is now being used to help treat diseases such as cancer. "It is important to treat emotional wounds as disorders because they really can hinder someone's reactions to the treatments, even someone's willingness to pursue treatment," Standiford explained. Of all his cancer patients, sixty-one percent have forgiveness issues and, of those, more than half are severe.

When we realize how much we have been forgiven by God, we find a sense of peace. Pray for those who have offended you and ask God to bless them. It is hard to do this, but you will start to see them in a different way. Remember, "Hurt people hurt people." We must be intentional about breaking this cycle. Matthew 5:44 KJV tells us, *Love your enemies, bless them that curse you, do good to them that hate you, and pray for them which despitefully use you, and persecute you.* Forgiveness is something we do for ourselves to get well and move on. To forgive is to set a prisoner free and then to realize the prisoner was you! Forgiveness brings freedom!

Step Three: Renewing your mind…focus on God's love

After you've forgiven from your heart, you will find healing, and are ready for the third step to pull down this stronghold—renewing your mind. You need to release the people who have hurt you once and for all. If you stop thinking about what was done to you and stop talking about it, the offense will eventually fade from your memory. When the devil tries to get you to start talking or thinking about it, "turn the channel" in your brain. Hebrews 12:15 reminds us of the importance of not allowing unforgiveness to grow, *See to it that no one falls short of God's grace; that no root of resentment springs up and causes trouble, and by it many be defiled.*

Cancel the debt people owe you from past offenses. Again, remember to not wait for an apology from your offender to forgive. Some people do not even know they hurt you or don't even care about it. Do not avenge yourself. Let God do it. Romans 12:19 speaks to this truth: *Beloved, never avenge yourselves, but leave the way open for God's wrath [and His judicial righteousness]; for it is written [in Scripture], "Vengeance is Mine, I will repay," says the Lord.*

Focus on God, not your past offenses. Renew you mind to His love for you—His love will heal you. Remember, you have an Abba Father who loves you unconditionally.

Self-evaluation questions

To uncover a stronghold of offense and unforgiveness, ask yourself these questions:

- Am I hanging on to an offense from the past, feeling justified because I was right, and the other person was wrong?

- Do I feel the need to share past offenses with others, feeling vindicated when others feel sorry for me?

- Is there someone in my life that I just cannot forgive?

- Am I waiting for an apology before I forgive someone?

- Have I experienced a broken heart and feel that I just can't get past it?

- Am I offended at God for prayers that weren't answered as I wanted?

- Do I feel that it is my responsibility to bring about justice from an offense?

Scriptures to pull down offense and unforgiveness

Believe and act on these scriptures to renew your mind on offense and unforgiveness:

"No weapon that is formed against you will succeed; And every tongue that rises against you in judgment you will condemn. This (peace, righteousness, security, and triumph over opposition) is the heritage of the servants of the Lord, And this is their vindication from me," says the Lord. —Isaiah 54:17

I do not consider, brethren, that I have captured and made it my own (yet); but one thing I do (it is my one aspiration): forgetting what lies behind and straining forward to what lies ahead. —Philippians 3:13

Do not (earnestly) remember the former things; neither consider the things of old. —Isaiah 43:18

He heals the broken in heart and binds up their wounds (curing their pain and sorrows). —Psalm 147:3

But I say to you, love [that is, unselfishly seek the best or higher good for] your enemies and pray for those who persecute you. —Matthew 5:44

Beloved, never avenge yourselves, but leave the way open for God's wrath [and His judicial righteousness]; for it is written [in Scripture], "Vengeance is Mine, I will repay," says the Lord. —Romans 12:19

Chapter Six
Lust and Sexual Impurities

The sins of lust and sexual defilement can sneak into someone's life with just a click on an electronic device and, if not dealt with, can destroy someone's future. For example, I once learned of a Bible college student who developed a problem through her iPhone. She became hooked on pornography and had great turmoil because she knew the Lord was calling her to be a pastor. She cried out to God and asked me for prayer. As it turned out, she would soon be leaving on a mission trip—an important step in her development as a minister. She agreed to leave her phone behind; so, for days during this mission trip, the temptation of pornography was not a problem. She simply could not access this door to sin in her life while she was away.

Additionally, she took the step of blocking all indecent pictures from her app on her phone. When she returned from her mission trip, she was able to stay free from lust and pornography. She went on to graduate and is now an associate pastor. What if she hadn't been proactive to remove this problem from her life? If not dealt with, these problems tend to get worse—not better—over time. Do you think she would have pushed on to become a pastor? Praise God, she took the necessary steps to get set free!

Understanding lust

Lust is defined as an intense or unbridled sexual desire and as an intense longing or craving. Lust in itself is a stronghold, leading to harmful feelings and causing people to behave destructively toward others. Lust also often leads to sins of sexual defilement. These sins include pornography, homosexuality, adultery, and fornication. All sexual sins cause problems, but I see so many people struggling with pornography and homosexuality that I will focus on these two issues for much of the chapter.

To better understand the power of lust, let's look at two examples of men in the Bible who faced temptations with it. The first man is Joseph, whose story is found in Genesis 39:7-10. His master's wife tried to seduce him, but Joseph chose to run – not just walk—away from this woman. Because he clung to his sexual purity, Joseph was able to achieve his destiny to become the second most powerful leader in Egypt, working closely with the Pharaoh. Joseph's story shows that God's grace will help you to resist sexual temptation if you will take it.

In contrast, Samson wanted his own will more than anything else. He gave in to his lust for women and became involved with several women who were not God's will for his life. Satan used these women to destroy his destiny. His story can be found in Judges 16:4-5.

We have to recognize that lust is a sin and a destructive sin at that. The world tries to tell us that lust, pornography, and other sexual impurities are normal. However, James 1:15 tells us the truth about lust, *Then when the illicit desire has conceived, it gives birth to sin; and when sin has run its course, it gives birth to death.* In contrast, God loves us and wants us to have the freedom found in purity, which is defined as freedom from evil or guilt; innocence; chastity.

Lust and pornography: secrets that destroy

As mentioned above, lust is sin which produces death. Often, Christians who are involved in lust and pornography try to hide their sin. Satan loves for you to cover up what you are doing and thinking in private. No one wants to talk about this "secret sin," but it is becoming more prevalent and we must talk about it. At a recent Christian conference, it was noted that nine out of ten of the 565 men in attendance said that lust, pornography, and fantasizing were issues that were disconnecting them in their relationship with God.

Remember the story at the beginning of this chapter? It's not just men who are being tempted. Women also need to be aware of issues with lust and pornography. Additionally, women may fall into snares with romance novels, TV shows, or movies as well. Many of them contain adultery, lust, fornication, and more, and can cause them to fantasize on impure thoughts.

Everyone is being tempted. It is just a click away on our televisions, phones, and other electronic devices. The devil works overtime to entice Christians to get them addicted to porn, lust, and the other sins they lead to. Allowing yourself to look at one sexually graphic picture starts the craving to see more. Ask people who have been trapped in pornography—it's addictive. Satan knows he can destroy your destiny if he can get you into secret, sexual sins.

Your level of sexual purity will determine not only your relationship with Christ, but it will also affect the doors God wants to open for you to minister. We all have heard of men and women who have fallen in ministry due to sexual immorality. As Doug Weiss says in his book, Clean, "If the devil can seduce you, then he can reduce you."

Another story of these secret sins causing terrible results in someone's life involves a prominent pastor, known all over the world for his passionate preaching. He had been in ministry for years when he was caught with a prostitute. It was all over the news. People were shocked. Afterwards, he went on television crying and apologizing for his behavior. It wasn't much later that he was caught again with another prostitute. This time, people were incredibly disappointed in him, and he lost everything. I happened to know some people who knew him quite well. They ended up ministering to him and said his problem came from pornography. He was saved as a young man, but he had been heavily into pornography and did not give it up when he became a Christian. His pride told him to keep it a secret until he was openly exposed. Unfortunately, all these secrets and lies ruined his ministry.

One of the best explanations that I know of for the stronghold of lust and pornography comes from the aforementioned, Doug Weiss, a counselor with years of experience in helping men with sexual impurity. He says, "U (you) + P (pornography) = D (destruction), but U (you) + C (getting clean) = L (life-giving positive fruit)." Doug goes on to further explain the destructiveness of this stronghold, "Fire is the best analogy for men and women who engage in ongoing and unchecked lust, pornography, masturbation, and other sexual behaviors not related to a spouse. Fire <u>contained</u> is a gift (it warms us, and you can cook with it), but in an <u>uncontained</u> situation, fire can wreak havoc and destroy and do great damage to our lives. Many women have come to me who were dating or married to men with a fire for pornography and lust. They refused to get help and counsel and this uncontained fire either broke their engagements or destroyed their marriages."

Lust and homosexuality

Several years ago, two prominent male pastors were exposed for immorality. One was exposed as having a homosexual affair. It was all over the national and international news. In the letter he wrote to the members of his church, he said that he thought he could handle his temptations with homosexuality. He went on to say it was his pride that kept him from getting help. Because of this, he lost his church and many other positions he held, as well as his priceless reputation forever. The devil effectively seduced and reduced this man.

The practice of homosexuality and its acceptance as an alternative lifestyle is becoming more prevalent in our society today. Nearly every day, we read and hear things which indicate that more people are accepting homosexuality as a normal behavior. For example:
- Ordinances have been passed which grant homosexuals and lesbians equal rights to practice and promote their "lifestyle."
- Gay churches have been established and gay priests and ministers have been ordained in many denominations.
- Many cities actually cater to the open display of homosexual behavior.

How should Christians react to all this? I believe it is our responsibility to openly and willingly face this problem. However, whatever the case may be, our approach should always be with love and tolerance.

What causes homosexuality? Experts—including psychologists, psychiatrists, scientists, and different religious leaders—are trying to find the real causes. The American Physiological Association website states, "There is no consensus among scientists about the exact reasons that an individual develops a heterosexual, bisexual, gay, or lesbian orientation. Although much research has examined the possible genetic, hormonal, developmental, social, and cultural influences on sexual orientation, no findings have emerged that permit scientists to conclude that sexual orientation is determined by any particular factor or factors. Many think that nature-nurture both play complex roles; most people experience little or no sense of choice about their sexual orientation."

Author and minister Tim LaHaye lists and describes the components for developing a predisposition to homosexuality. Please carefully note that the components listed below do not cause one to become a homosexual; rather, they can contribute to the development of a predisposition toward homosexuality. A person can (and many do) have all these components and still not be a homosexual. According to LaHaye, the components include:
- Melancholy temperament
- Inadequate parental relationships
- Permissive childhood training
- Insecurity about sexual identity
- Childhood sexual trauma
- Early interest in sex
- Youthful masturbator and sexual fantasizer
- Childhood associates and peer pressure

What are the real causes of homosexuality? While I have great respect for scientists, such as those with the American Physiological Association, in their research, I strongly believe that Satan stands behind every move that nurtures homosexuality. He is the force behind the components listed by LaHaye and other factors that lead to this sin.

Satan and identity theft

Let's examine how Satan is the force behind homosexuality. People who are involved in the homosexual lifestyle are often seeking an identity. They don't know their identity, so they are constantly looking for one. We know that Satan's first strategy to deceive people is to get them to question their identity and, if possible, steal it. If Satan is successful in stealing your identity, then he can deliberately assign a new one to you. The concept of identity theft originates with Satan, who in heaven attempted to steal God's identity as he said, *I will make myself like the Most High.* (Isaiah 14:14)

Additionally, we see Satan trying to steal identity at other times in the Bible. In the Garden of Eden, he suggested to Eve that she could transcend her allegedly defective and restrictive (do not touch, do not eat) God-given identity by his offer of a new and improved identity, saying to her, *You will be like God.* (Genesis 3:5) Matthew 4:1-13 tells the story of how Satan even tried to tempt Jesus with the issue of identity. In the temptations in the wilderness, Satan challenged Jesus by saying that—if He was really the Son of God—He should prove it by performing miracles like jumping off the pinnacle of the temple or turning stones into bread.

While hanging on the cross, Jesus again heard through the Roman soldiers a final attack on his identity, *If you are [really] the King of the Jews, save Yourself [from death]!* (Luke 23:37) You can bet that Satan was behind this assault on Jesus' identity. However, Jesus did not accept Satan's attacks on His identity, but instead knew the truth.

All this shows a great deal about how personal identity has the power to shape human conduct. Satan is not too troubled should we focus on overcoming a whole list of outwardly sinful behaviors, but he trembles in fear when we discover our true identity in Christ. Why? Because the internalization of our God-given identity through genuine worship provides the programming that breaks the power of Satan over us. Here are some important facts to consider about Satan's character:

He is the father of lies. (John 8:44)
He is known as the thief. (John 10:10)
He is a deceiver, manipulator, and appears as an angel of light. (2 Corinthians 11:14)
He is the author of confusion. (1 Corinthians 14:33)

As a liar, thief, deceiver, manipulator, and one who causes confusion, Satan seeks to attack your identity and stop you from fulfilling God's will for your life. But his lies are nothing when you know your identity in Christ and who God made you to be.

Is homosexuality something people are born with or can it be overcome?

Is it possible to overcome homosexuality? Those who believe that homosexuality is "something you are born with" would take great issue with the idea that it is possible to change or otherwise overcome homosexuality. However, there are at least two compelling reasons that convince me that it is possible.

The first reason why I believe it is possible is because, unfortunately, the scientific arena is one that can be easily tainted by presuppositions or political correctness, and sometimes even religious correctness. For this reason, it will be a long time before adequate research can be done that will come close to resolving this issue conclusively. But research from impartial sources has indicated that it is possible to overcome homosexuality. Masters and Johnson, well-known researchers in human sexuality, reported in their book, Homosexuality in Perspective, a 67% success rate in helping homosexuals revert to heterosexual behavior. Also, in an article published in the American Journal of Psychiatry, E. Mansell Pattison, M.D., and Myrna Loy Pattison, from the Department of Psychiatry and Health Behavior, Medical College of Georgia, documented eleven cases of men who claim to have changed their sexual orientation from exclusively homosexual to exclusive heterosexual through involvement in a church fellowship.

This leads to the second reason why I believe it is possible to overcome homosexuality—the biblical evidence. In writing to the church at Corinth, a city known for its immorality, Paul warns them, *Do you not know that the unrighteous will not inherit or have any share in the kingdom of God? Do not be deceived; neither the sexually immoral, nor idolaters, nor adulterers, nor effeminate (by perversion), nor those who participate in homosexuality, nor thieves, nor the greedy, nor drunkards, nor revilers (whose words are used as weapons to abuse, insult, humiliate, intimidate, or slander), nor swindlers will inherit or have any share in the kingdom of God.* (1 Corinthians 6:9-10)

Notice that in the above verses, Paul included homosexuality as conduct that can keep one out of the kingdom of God. But then Paul says something that should give great hope to those who are willing to believe that it is possible to overcome homosexuality: *And such were some of you [before you believed]. But you were washed [by the atoning sacrifice of Christ], you were sanctified [set apart for God, and made holy], you were justified [declared free of guilt] in the name of the Lord Jesus Christ and in the [Holy] Spirit of our God [the source of the believer's new life and changed behavior].* (1 Corinthians 6:11) Through the blood of Jesus Christ, and the power of the Holy Spirit, it is possible for a homosexual to be forgiven and to be sanctified (set apart for a holy purpose)!

However, while it is possible to overcome homosexuality, it is not necessarily easy. As with all sin, forgiveness can be received immediately when united with Christ in His death through baptism. But living the kind of "sanctified" life required of all Christians is one that requires a transformation which occurs in time as we submit our minds and bodies to the transforming and strengthening power of the Holy Spirit!

Step One: Admit your problem

Problems of sexual defilement, such as pornography, lust, homosexuality, adultery, fornication and more are often kept hidden. However, as mentioned earlier, these secret sins are destroying people from the inside out. You must recognize that no matter what the world says, these behaviors are not normal and are not healthy. No amount of pornography or any other sexual sin is okay. Remember, a stronghold exerts control over your behavior. So, with a stronghold of sexual defilement, you will feel as if you have lost control over choices you make in regard to your physical desires. You've got to admit your problem to eliminate this stronghold from your life.

Don't make excuses. In particular, don't use the excuse that God's grace and unconditional love cover sins of lust, pornography, and other sexual immorality. Romans 6:1-2 reminds us, What shall we say [to all this]? Should we continue in sin and practice sin as a habit so that [God's gift of] grace may increase and overflow? Certainly not! How can we, the very ones who died to sin, continue to live in it any longer.

We need to be honest and confess our sins as 1 John 1:9 says, *If we [freely] admit that we have sinned and confess our sins, He is faithful and just [true to His own nature and promises], and will forgive our sins and cleanse us continually from all unrighteousness [our wrongdoing, everything not in conformity with His will and purpose]*. Admitting and confessing this problem is the beginning of how to get free from the stronghold of sexual impurities. Counseling, prayer, and accountability may also be necessary. Many Christians are stuck in the trap of lust, pornography, and other sexual immorality because of one thing—pride. People, especially those in ministry, don't want anyone to think less of them, so they keep these sins hidden. However, it is only after the darkness (sexual impurity) is exposed to the light, that freedom starts to come.

Step Two: Find the root

Sadly, sins of sexual defilement sometimes enter people's lives during childhood. Tragically, some children are sexually abused. Others may have been exposed to inappropriate material at an early age. It is painful to go back to these roots, but in doing so, you will be able to gain freedom, if you are willing to forgive.

For others, you may have been exposed to indecent images or videos while online and the problem escalated. And there are a myriad of other ways this stronghold can enter your life. You will have to take steps to remove this root from your life, as the Bible college student at the beginning of this chapter did. Again, you can be free, but you've got to remove the problem from the root, and you can't do that unless you recognize how a stronghold with lust or sexual defilement first entered your life.

Step Three: Be renewed

The strongholds of lust and sexual impurity take a powerful grip on people both emotionally and physically—it truly has a strong hold on people. They don't just go away because you want them to, but it can be done. Throughout the rest of this chapter, I'll give you scriptures to renew your mind on these strongholds, help you understand your true identity in Christ—as well as practical steps to help you remain in victory.

Be an overcomer!

As suggested previously, it is possible for a person to overcome his or her homosexuality and other sins of sexual impurity even if he or she is not a Christian. However, so much more help is available if a person is willing to come to Jesus Christ and the transforming power of the Holy Spirit! In the following section, we'll briefly examine the positive steps one can take in dealing with the sins of lust and homosexuality. Here are the six keys to overcoming homosexuality and sexual impurity:

1. **Obey Jesus Christ as Savior and Lord.** Being obedient to Jesus means repenting of your sins. The power of repentance is seen in Acts 2:38, *Repent [change your old way of thinking, turn from your sinful ways, accept and follow Jesus as the Messiah] and be baptized, each of you, in the name of Jesus Christ because of the forgiveness of your sins; and you will receive the gift of the Holy Spirit.* Romans 8:11-13 shows us the power that we have in Jesus, *And if the Spirit of Him who raised Jesus from the dead lives in you, He who raised Christ Jesus from the dead will also give life to your mortal bodies through His Spirit, who lives in you. So then, brothers and sisters, we have an obligation, but not to our flesh [our human nature, our worldliness, our*

sinful capacity], to live according to the [impulses of the] flesh [our nature without the Holy Spirit]— for if you are living according to the [impulses of the] flesh, you are going to die. But if [you are living] by the [power of the Holy] Spirit you are habitually putting to death the sinful deeds of the body, you will [really] live forever. Yes, it is by the Spirit that you are able to *put to death the deeds of the body*, for as Paul wrote to the Ephesians, it is through the Spirit that God strengthens your inward man: *to be strengthened and spiritually energized with power through His Spirit in your inner self, [indwelling your innermost being and personality].* (Ephesians 3:16) With such "divine help" we are able to do whatever the will of God calls us to do. As Paul wrote in his epistle to the Philippians, *For it is [not your strength, but it is] God who is effectively at work in you, both to will and to work [that is, strengthening, energizing, and creating in you the longing and the ability to fulfill your purpose] for His good pleasure,* (Philippians 2:13), and *I can do all things [which He has called me to do] through Him who strengthens and empowers me [to fulfill His purpose—I am self-sufficient in Christ's sufficiency; I am ready for anything and equal to anything through Him who infuses me with inner strength and confident peace.]* (Philippians 4:13). When you obey Christ and submit your life to Him, you are not alone in your struggle against sin and the temptations you often face in the flesh; by the spirit of God, you can receive the strength Christ provides!

2. **Restrict what goes into your mind.** Jesus pointed out in His Sermon on the Mount that the problem of adultery actually begins in the heart (mind), *but I say to you that everyone who [so much as] looks at a woman with lust for her has already committed adultery with her in his heart.* (Matthew 5:28) The same can be said for homosexuality. Therefore, people who are serious in their efforts to overcome any sexual sin must be careful about what they allow into their minds. In Romans 8:5, Paul warned that Christians should not be focused on their flesh, *For those who are living according to the flesh set their minds on the things of the flesh [which gratify the body], but those who are living according to the Spirit, [set their minds on] the things of the Spirit [His will and purpose].* If a person is going to be truly transformed, it will occur only when the mind is being

renewed, and he becomes the living sacrifice that Paul wrote of in Romans 12:1 NKJV, *I beseech you therefore, brethren, by the mercies of God, that you present your bodies a living sacrifice, holy, acceptable to God, which is your reasonable service.* And again, we remember Romans 12:2 NKJV, *Do not be conformed to this world, but be transformed by the renewing of your mind, that you may prove what is that good and acceptable and perfect will of God.* A person's mind cannot be renewed if he allows himself to dwell on those things that will prompt lustful desires. Rather, he needs to heed the following admonition, *Whatever things are true, whatever things are noble, whatever things are just, whatever things are pure, whatever things are lovely, whatever things are of good report, if there is any virtue and if there is anything praiseworthy—meditate on these things.* (Philippians 4:8 NKJV) Rather than dwelling on things that will weaken his resolve, a person committed to overcoming temptations of the flesh will devote his thoughts, his reading, his television, and movie viewing to such things as described above!

3. **Avoid unhealthy friends and hangouts.** You should be aware of the dangers of the wrong kind of companionship, *Do not be deceived: "Bad company corrupts good morals."* (1 Corinthians 15:33). Friends can be a wonderful blessing, but the wrong kind of friends can be a disaster! Avoid like the plague those who would entice you back into sin. And avoid those environments where the opportunities for temptations are great, where homosexuals are known to frequent. In other words, *clothe yourselves with the Lord Jesus Christ, and make no provision for [nor even think about gratifying] the flesh in regard to its improper desires.* (Romans 13:14) Do not provide opportunities for the flesh to be tempted to give in to unrighteous desires!

4. **Become active in the local church.** Once you have been delivered, you need encouragement from Christian fellowship. The very purpose of Christian assemblies is to provide such, as described in Hebrews 10:24-25, *Let us consider [thoughtfully] how we may encourage one another to love and to do good deeds, not forsaking our meeting together [as believers for worship and instruction], as is the habit of some, but encouraging one another; and all the more [faithfully] as you see the day [of Christ's return] approaching.*

Of course, it is essential that those struggling with trying to overcome sexual sins be fully accepted—despite their pasts—by their fellow Christians, or they will be terribly discouraged! It is the Lord's desire that local congregations be havens for all who seek to serve the Lord and to overcome sin.

5. **Believe in God for an unlimited future!** It is important to remember that with God nothing is impossible! The Scriptures tell us that God is able to do things beyond what we are able to imagine: *Now to Him who is able to [carry out His purpose and] do superabundantly more than all that we dare ask or think [infinitely beyond our greatest prayers, hopes, or dreams], according to His power that is at work within us.* (Ephesians 3:20). Notice the superlatives used by Paul (exceedingly, abundantly, above all). We soon get the impression that this "power" that works in us is really beyond description! But it is available to those who commit themselves to serving the Lord! Not only that, but we have the promise that God will never allow us to be tempted beyond what we are able to handle as 1 Corinthians 10:13 says, *No temptation [regardless of its source] has overtaken or enticed you that is not common to human experience [nor is any temptation unusual or beyond human resistance]; but God is faithful [to His word—He is compassionate and trustworthy], and He will not let you be tempted beyond your ability [to resist], but along with the temptation He [has in the past and is now and] will [always] provide the way out as well, so that you will be able to endure it [without yielding, and will overcome temptation with joy].* With the power of God working in us to give us strength, and the providence of God working around us to keep us out of temptations beyond our ability to overcome, we can change and be all that God wants us to be!

6. **Finally, pray! Yes, pray!** First Thessalonians 5:17 tells us to *be unceasing and persistent in prayer*. Whenever the temptation is great, pray. Why pray? The author of Hebrews gives us two good reasons: mercy and grace. Hebrews 4:16 tells us, *Therefore let us [with privilege] approach the throne of grace [that is, the throne of God's gracious favor] with confidence and without fear, so that we may receive mercy [for our failures] and find [His amazing] grace to help in time of need [an appropriate blessing, coming just at the right*

moment]. This verse shows us that through prayer we can receive from God both mercy and grace to help us in time of need. Mercy for the times when we do not take advantage of the help God provides, and grace to help in those times when we do seek to take advantage of it. Through prayer, the Word, the help of the brethren, and the Holy Spirit Himself, anyone (including the homosexual and lesbian) should be able to say with the apostle Paul, *I can do all things through Christ who strengthens me.* (Philippians 4:13 NKJV)

As previously discussed, transformation takes work. Refusing to let strongholds control your life takes committing, with God's help, to pull them down and out of your life. It also takes courage and time. You can go to a counselor for help in identifying the problems that are hurting you or holding you back in life, but it still takes your cooperation to demolish them. The Bible says to not just be hearers of the Word but doers of it. (James 1:22) Additionally, you must transform and renew your mind as commanded in Romans 12:2 by replacing the world's views and actions with what the Word says.

May God give you whatever portion of that strength you need!

An example of an overcomer

Doug Weiss, the man I referred to earlier in the chapter, has a counseling service devoted to people who have problems with sexual lust, pornography, and immorality. He is an amazing example of someone who has overcome the stronghold of lust. He started his counseling service because, for years, he himself had problems with lust and pornography. In his book, Clean, Doug gives his steps to freedom from sexual impurity. He says the most critical step for him to be set free from this stronghold was revealing his secret to his roommate in seminary. Doug says, "If you don't confess your sin to another man or woman, you can try to get free, but you will fail!"

Doug has been **sexually pure** and free from lust and pornography for years. Here are the steps he used to renew his

mind and gain freedom from this stronghold:
1. He humbled himself.
2. He confessed his sexual sin to another man.
3. He repented.
4. He had blocks put on his Internet access.
5. He became accountable to another man, and later to his wife.

Final thoughts on the stronghold of sexual impurities

God's love is unconditional, but He hates sexual sin and perversion. He doesn't want this stronghold to choke you or cause you to hurt others. The Bible is loaded with scriptures that warn us about sexual temptations. First Corinthians 6:9 sums it up when it says the impure and immoral will not inherit the kingdom of God. God's heart is 100% for you. He wants every hindering chain to be broken off your life. You hold the key. Will you continue to conceal it or will you reveal it to someone and commit to sexual purity? Keep in mind, God gives you weapons to protect yourself from sexual temptations, including:
1. The fear (respect) of the Lord.
2. His Word and what it says about sexual immorality.
3. Honesty—admitting you have a problem with lust, pornography, etc.
4. Talking to another man or woman about it.
5. Being accountable to someone.
6. Setting pornography blocks such as "Covenant Eyes" on your Internet service.

And always remember Proverbs 23:7 KJV, *For as he thinketh in his heart, so is he.* You will think about what you see on television, in movies, and other things you allow yourself to look at. These things will affect your life and cause you to lust and fall into sexual immorality. You will never stop the enemy's plan to destroy you with lust and pornography if you continue to embrace it through your choices. For some, a prayer of deliverance will immediately break the spirit of lust and pornography. For others, it will take counseling, accountability, and "rewiring" of the brain just as a drug addict has to do.

If you don't <u>humble</u> yourself before God, eventually you will face <u>humiliation</u>. Be proactive. God wants to help you, but He needs your cooperation. I wrote this chapter on the stronghold of sexual impurities, not to bring shame or condemnation, but to let you know you are not alone. Second Corinthians 10:5 says to bring into captivity every thought to the obedience of Christ. Together with Him, you can get the victory!

Self-evaluation questions

To help you determine if you struggle with strongholds of lust or sexual impurity, ask yourself these questions:

- Do I have the attitude that what I do in the privacy of my home is my own business?

- Do I make the excuse that sins of lust and pornography don't matter because of God's grace and forgiveness?

- Do I think a small amount of pornography is acceptable?

- Do I feel uncertain about my identity and have questions about who I am, especially sexually?

- Am I involved in sexual impurity—pornography, homosexuality, adultery—but keep it secret from everyone?

- Am I scared that my relationships and/or career would be ruined if anyone found out about my double life?

Scriptures to pull down the strongholds of lust and sexual impurities

Renew your mind by meditating and acting on these scriptures:

But clothe yourselves with the Lord Jesus Christ, and make no provision for [nor even think about gratifying] the flesh in regard to its improper desires. —Romans 13:14

And if the Spirit of him who raised Jesus from the dead is living in you, he who raised Christ from the dead will also give life to your mortal bodies because of his Spirit who lives in you. Therefore, brothers and sisters, we have an obligation—but it is not to the flesh, to live according to it. For if you live according to the flesh, you will die; but if by the Spirit you put to death the misdeeds of the body, you will live. —Romans 8:11-13

If we [freely] admit that we have sinned and confess our sins, He is faithful and just [true to His own nature and promises], and will forgive our sins and cleanse us continually from all unrighteousness [our wrongdoing, everything not in conformity with His will and purpose]. —1 John 1:9

Finally, believers, whatever is true, whatever is honorable and worthy of respect, whatever is right and confirmed by God's word, whatever is pure and wholesome, whatever is lovely and brings peace, whatever is admirable and of good repute; if there is any excellence, if there is anything worthy of praise, think continually on these things [center your mind on them, and implant them in your heart]. —Philippians 4:8

Now to Him who is able to [carry out His purpose and] do superabundantly more than all that we dare ask or think [infinitely beyond our greatest prayers, hopes, or dreams], according to His power that is at work within us. —Ephesians 3:20

Therefore let us [with privilege] approach the throne of grace [that is, the throne of God's gracious favor] with confidence and without fear, so that we may receive mercy [for our failures] and find [His amazing] grace to help in time of need [an appropriate blessing, coming just at the right moment]. —Hebrews 4:16

Chapter Seven
Pride, Rebellion, and Lying

Several years ago, we took a mission team to the Dominican Republic, including five teenage boys who had never ministered before. One was my son. At first, these boys were very timid and shy when they shared their testimonies and ministered. As the people positively responded, they relaxed and started getting more confident. However, they let their positive experiences go past confidence and go to their heads instead. One night, we let them lay hands on the people that came up for prayer. After the meeting, I heard my son and one other boy asking, "How many did you get to fall down?" One boy answered, "I got five," and another said, "Oh, I did better than that. I got eight."

These boys were just strutting around like teenage peacocks. They didn't see that pride was taking over, and that they were taking the glory for what had happened. We had a "come to Jesus" meeting afterwards and they realized then what they were doing. I laid hands on them, and the Holy Spirit let them know that it was Him who did the "slaying in the Spirit." It was as if He tackled these boys like a football player and for at least twenty minutes none of them could move or get up off the floor. They will never forget that lesson from the Holy Ghost.

Jesus said He would not share His glory with anyone. Isaiah 42:8 says, *I am the Lord, that is My Name; My glory I will not give to another, Nor My praise to carved idols.* When people get prideful about their ministries or their life's accomplishments, it is because they have forgotten that the source of all they accomplish is God and He alone deserves the glory. In the story above, the teen boys submitted to the Holy Spirit, preventing a stronghold of pride from developing. Unfortunately, not everyone takes this step and pride becomes a real issue in their lives.

Understanding pride

Pride has been the downfall of many past and contemporary ministers, leaders, and people of influence. Pride is defined as a high or inordinate (not normal) opinion of one's own dignity, importance, merit, or superiority. People with a stronghold of pride may be seen in all facets of society, from churches to the business arena. Most of the time, people do not even see how prideful or conceited they have become.

The Bible contains 43 scriptures that speak of the negative consequences of allowing pride in your life. Pride is deceptive and can come upon you without your realizing it. That is why you must be submitted and accountable to someone who can be your check and balance to tell you if you are getting puffed up with pride.

One scripture that warns of the negative consequences of pride is Proverbs 29:23: *A man's pride and sense of self-importance will bring him down, But he who has a humble spirit will obtain honor.* An example of this happening is found in Acts 12:23 when an angel struck down Herod because he did not give God the glory—subsequently, he was eaten by worms and died.

Pride is one of Satan's greatest tools to destroy a person, especially one who is serving the Lord. Satan is a good example of pride. He started out, we assume, as a humble, anointed cherub, but because he let pride take over, he fell. The Lord spoke the following rebuke to Lucifer in Ezekiel 28:15, 17-19, *You were blameless in your ways from the day you were created until unrighteousness and evil were found in you...Your heart was proud and arrogant because of your beauty; You destroyed your wisdom for the sake of your splendor. I cast you to the ground; I lay you before kings, that they might look at you...All the people (nations) who knew you are appalled at you; You have come to a horrible and terrifying end and will forever cease to be.*

Besides Satan, there are numerous other examples in the Bible of people who fell because of their pride, including Naaman (2 Kings 5:11-13), Hezekiah (2 Kings 20:13), Haman (Esther 3:5), and Nebuchadnezzar (Daniel 4:30-34).

Unfortunately, many church leaders in recent history have fallen because of pride. Most of them started out humbly, but—as they got attention, more miracles occurred, and their ministries grew—they succumbed to pride and began to take all the glory.

Pride also hurts your personal relationships. It can keep you from seeing and saying, "I was wrong," or "I am sorry." It can stop you from forgiving others. It keeps you from seeing and acknowledging your weaknesses. Once, when I was teaching my course on pulling down strongholds at a Bible college, a woman in the class declared that she had none—even after we had studied all 16 topics. No one—but her—thought so. Regrettably, pride tends to drive others away—relationships are strained when pride issues are present.

Pride...door to rebellion

Pride can keep you from obeying God because you think you are special or exempt. Therefore, pride sometimes leads people into rebellion. You can think you are "above" the law and do not have to answer to anyone but yourself, allowing rebellion into your heart. What exactly is rebellion? Rebellion is refusing to follow ordinary guidelines, resisting control or correction, and unruliness.

At the Bible college where I teach, most of the students are cooperative. However, our Dean of Students would tell you of the many students that he has suspended and even dismissed because they wanted to do things their way. Unfortunately, these students did not heed James 1:22, *But prove yourselves doers of the word (actively and continually obeying God's precepts), and not merely listeners (who hear the word, but fail to internalize its meaning), deluding yourselves (by unsound reasoning contrary to the truth).* I am amazed at how many people call themselves Christians and yet do the opposite of what is in the Word.

I've had to work on the stronghold of rebellion myself. When I first got saved after being in a strict boarding school, I had developed a real habit of doing what I wanted regardless of the rules. I did not want to change, but as I read the Word and in particular, Hebrews 13:17, *Obey your [spiritual] leaders and submit to them [recognizing their authority over you], for they are keeping watch over your souls and continually guarding your spiritual welfare as those who will give an account [of their stewardship of you]. Let them do this with joy and not with grief and groans, for this would be of no benefit to you*, I knew the rebellious attitude had to go—and with the Lord's help, it has.

A good example of a man in the Bible who started out humble but fell into pride and rebellion is King Saul. At first, when the prophet Samuel gave him orders from the Lord, he followed them. But then he began to practice "selective obedience." Saul thought his plan was a better plan than God's. Sound familiar? Submission to authority goes against our carnal, selfish nature, but we must overcome it, because it is a very serious offense to God. Many of us are tempted to do the same thing when the Word of the Lord speaks to us about doing something and we decide to do it "our way" or "part way."

Unfortunately, Saul did not overcome his carnal nature. Samuel told King Saul to completely destroy the Amalekites as the Lord had commanded. Saul decided it was better if he spared their king and some of the animals to offer as a sacrifice. Saul lied to Samuel and told him that he had completed the Lord's commands entirely. The Lord was not happy and told Samuel that Saul had not performed His commandments and was grieved that He had even made him king. Saul's behavior showed that pride and rebellion had overtaken him, prompting Samuel to reprimand him, *Has the Lord as great a delight in burnt offerings and sacrifices as in obedience to the voice of the Lord? Behold, to obey is better than sacrifice, And to heed [is better] than the fat of rams. For rebellion is as [serious as] the sin of divination (fortune-telling), And disobedience is as [serious as] false religion and idolatry. Because you have rejected the word of the Lord, He also has rejected you as king.* (1 Samuel 15:22-23) God rejected him, and he committed suicide.

God will not promote those who, like King Saul, are not submissive and obedient. Great men and women of God, when asked the reason for their longevity, responded that it was their obedience. Abraham is an example of complete obedience as a hearer and doer of the Word of God. In Genesis 22:1-8, he was told to sacrifice and kill his only son whom he had waited so long to have. Because of his sacrifice of complete obedience in taking the steps God had commanded, God spared his son. Abraham was made the "father of many nations" (Genesis 22:16-17), in contrast to King Saul who was dethroned.

If you want authority over Satan, you must obey the Word. Do as James 4:17 KJV says, *Submit yourselves therefore to God. Resist the devil, and he will flee from you.*

Lying, an epidemic we must avoid

Lying is another stronghold to be aware of. Lying is a big problem in the world and is becoming very common, even among Christians. In the above story about King Saul, we can see that lying—as he confidently told the prophet Samuel that he had followed the Lord's orders to completely destroy the Amalekites and all they owned—was part of his attitude of pride and rebellion. King Saul somehow justified the fact that it was okay to lie because he thought it would be good to spare their king and some of their best animals. Saul was putting his standards above the Lord's.

What is lying? It is defined as making a false statement with the intent to deceive, a false impression, an intentional untruth. Lying is an epidemic in these times, and we can all say that we have participated in a lie and, if not, we have at least been tempted to do so.

So, why do we lie? Many times, lying is easier than telling the truth. Additionally, we may lie to get unjust rewards, to get power or attention, to cover up a transgression, to make ourselves look better, to manipulate others, to hurt other people; the list goes on and on. And, yes, one lie usually leads to another.

Lies are a part of life—we hear them every day, starting with our leaders. Former presidents have lied and several were caught and either resigned or were impeached. Every day in the news or on television, we hear conflicting stories and many times it's difficult to discern who is telling the truth. We are clearly told in Colossians 3:9, *Do not lie to one another, for you have stripped off the old self with its evil practices.* The Lord takes lying very seriously. In Ephesians 4:25 we are again warned not to lie, *Therefore, rejecting all falsehood (whether lying, defrauding, telling half-truths, spreading rumors, any such as these), speak truth each one with his neighbor, for we are all parts of one another (and we are all parts of the body of Christ).*

Revelation 21:8 tells us that liars, along with a list of other people in sin, shall have their part in the lake that blazes with fire and brimstone. To the Lord, as He showed us with King Saul, lying is a serious problem. We must not take lying lightly but, instead, be obedient in telling the truth.

Step One: Facing pride, rebellion, and lying

To pull down the strongholds of pride, rebellion, and lying, you must first admit your problem. Take an honest look at your habits and behaviors. Does it seem that you have no control over telling lies; that you lie without thinking about it? Do you find yourself rebelling against those in authority? Additionally, if you find that others tell you they think you might have issues with pride, or if you consistently have relationship problems, you need to acknowledge the problem and pull down this stronghold. Be accountable to others and listen when they tell you that they see one or more of these strongholds in you.

Step Two: Get to the root of the problem

As with other strongholds, the next step to pulling down pride, rebellion, or lying is to get to the root of the problem. Ask the Lord to show you the point at which these negative habits began in your heart. Did you start telling lies during your youth, enjoying the perceived benefits? Maybe you received praise or attention for something you did or for your God-given talents, and you allowed that praise to go to your head with the result of developing pride. Or, maybe you've let rebellion become part of your identity, perhaps as a habit, for attention, or to punish someone. Just ask God to show you, so that you can eliminate these strongholds from the root.

Step Three: Renewal through clothing yourself in humility

The last step in pulling down the stronghold of pride is to renew your mind to the truth in God's Word—this means you walk in humility. Jesus was our example of complete humility, which is the opposite of pride. First Peter 5:5 says, *Clothe yourselves in humility toward one another (tie on the servant's apron), for God is opposed to the proud (the disdainful, the presumptuous, and He defeats them), but He gives grace to the humble.* There are many examples of people who have held important positions, yet have managed to keep their honor, humility, and reputation. To me, former President Ronald Reagan came across as a very humble man. Many times, he talked about prayer and his dependence on God. I remember watching him on television one night as he was in the Oval Office and walked over to a wall where Psalm 121 (which tells us that our help comes from the Lord) was displayed. Billy Graham is another person whom people honored and respected because of his gentle and humble spirit. Mother Teresa, whom I met personally, greeted us in India with total humility. Her life was that of a servant to the "poorest of the poor," as she called them. There are many others both in the secular and ministerial world who have exemplified humility. Their simple secret to longevity was walking in obedience to God and remaining humble. We must renew our mind on humility to pull down the stronghold of pride.

Most people who fall to pride have no accountability. They think they know more than anyone else, or they surround themselves with "yes men and women" who are afraid to stand up and warn them of the pride they see. Sadly, this type of behavior does not help people, but ultimately hurts them.

When it comes to pulling down the stronghold of lying, the Word says that even if lying is a deep-rooted habit from your past, you can overcome it. Colossians 3:10 tells us to clothe ourselves with *the new (spiritual) self who is being continually renewed in true knowledge in the image of Him who created the new self.* Before you were born again and your conscience was dead, you could justify and easily tell lies. Now that you have the "truth" in you, your spirit man "alarm" should go off and check you when you feel a lie coming on. Everyone is going to be tempted on a regular basis. Why? Remember, John 8:44 states that the devil is the father of all lies and all that is false—he is always ready to tempt you to lie.

However, if you slip and tell a lie or if false exaggeration comes out of your mouth, your Father is more than ready to forgive you. This is why it is good to have a time to reflect over your day and be accountable for your actions. You can't change your behavior if you don't take the time to evaluate it. Ask the Lord to give you the strength to tell the truth. If you are threatened or feel insecure, you can easily feel justified in lying; however, this isn't right, and you need to take those feelings to the Lord.

The Lord is more than able and willing to change and stop the habit of lying in you. When I first got saved, I didn't realize what a habit of "little white lies" I had as I justified them. It took time, and some days, I failed, but He has helped me to catch myself when I find it easier to lie than to tell the truth.

The Lord will help you overcome the stronghold of rebellion as well. As mentioned previously, grasping the truth of Hebrews 13:17 will help you as it did me, *Obey your [spiritual] leaders and submit to them [recognizing their authority over you], for they are keeping watch over your souls and continually guarding your spiritual welfare as those who will give an account [of their stewardship of you]. Let them do this with joy and not with grief and groans, for this would be of no benefit to you.* Remember that you are a new creation in Christ and that the Holy Spirit is guiding you. Each day, ask for His help to submit to godly authorities.

Self-evaluation questions

To check for strongholds of pride, rebellion, and lying, ask yourself these questions:

- Do people tell me they see pride in me, even if I can't see it myself?

- Do I consistently have relationship problems?

- Do I have a sense of superiority when I compare myself to others? Do I give myself, rather than God, credit for my gifts and successes?

- Do I prefer to surround myself with people who never challenge me, but instead agree with everything I say?

- Do I struggle with submitting to those in authority? Do I tend to have rebellious feelings and actions toward authority?

- Do I feel that because of past offenses toward me, I am justified in being rebellious? Am I wanting to punish people because of the hurts I've experienced?

- Do I tend to get involved in gossip, even if it means exaggerating truth and lying about others?

- Is lying a habit that I just can't seem to break?

- Do I lie to get rewards, attention, power, to cover up my past, or to control others in my life?

Scriptures to pull down the strongholds of pride, rebellion, and lying

Use these scriptures to renew your mind and pull down pride, rebellion, and lying:

A man's pride and sense of self-importance will bring him down, But he who has a humble spirit will obtain honor. —Proverbs 29:23

Obey your [spiritual] leaders and submit to them [recognizing their authority over you], for they are keeping watch over your souls and continually guarding your spiritual welfare as those who will give an account [of their stewardship of you]. Let them do this with joy and not with grief and groans, for this would be of no benefit to you. —Hebrews 13:17

So submit to [the authority of] God. Resist the devil [stand firm against him] and he will flee from you. —James 4:7

Do not lie to one another, for you have stripped off the old self with its evil practices. —Colossians 3:9

Therefore, rejecting all falsehood [whether lying, defrauding, telling half-truths, spreading rumors, any such as these], speak truth each one with his neighbor, for we are all parts of one another [and we are all parts of the body of Christ]. —Ephesians 4:25

Likewise, you younger men [of lesser rank and experience], be subject to your elders [seek their counsel]; and all of you, clothe yourselves with humility toward one another [tie on the servant's apron], for God is opposed to the proud [the disdainful, the presumptuous, and He defeats them], but He gives grace to the humble. —1 Peter 5:5

Chapter Eight
Anger

A situation with anger that you can all relate to is road rage. Satan uses people or circumstances to provoke you into anger— and road rage is a perfect example of this. One day, I was innocently driving through the Garden of the Gods Park in Colorado, when I drove around a curve and approached an intersection in which the other driver had a yield sign. When I saw her, I slowed down and kept driving, completely following the rules of the road. The next thing I knew, the other driver had put down her window and yelled at me and used some offensive sign language and barely missed hitting my car—simply because she did not see the yield sign.

Should having someone cross in front of you cause an outrage? Apparently, she thought so. In return, I found myself getting angry. What right did she have to act this way? However, I stopped my anger and asked the Lord to help me. Despite the other driver's irate behavior, I was able to exercise self-control. Thank God, I had the Father of self-control living inside me.

In this story, I was able to overcome my feelings of anger with the help of the Holy Spirit. However, for some people, anger is so deeply ingrained in them that situations such as these cause them to explode with rage. In this case, a stronghold of anger is often the cause.

Understanding anger

What is anger? It is a reaction to any real or imagined insult, frustration, or injustice. It is an emotion that you can control, but when it is a stronghold, it usually controls you. If you have several strongholds, such as jealousy, rejection, low self-esteem, or unforgiveness, it is easy to walk around as an angry person. If you were raised by angry parents or have suffered verbal or sexual or physical abuse, anger could be a by-product.

Why do you need to deal with anger issues? The Bible warns about anger in Psalm 37:8, *Cease from anger and abandon wrath; Do not fret; it leads only to evil.* Tragically, anger often spirals into destructive behavior, such as emotional outbursts and even violence. Furthermore, Psalm 4:4 tells us, *Tremble (with anger or fear), and do not sin.* The Bible says that, as a believer in Christ, you have to relinquish your emotions over to the leading of the Holy Spirit. You will have the power to control your emotions through the power of Jesus within you if you allow Him to help you.

Right from the beginning of time, man has had problems with anger. In Genesis chapter four, we have an example of someone who fell into Satan's trap of using people or circumstances to provoke anger. Remember Cain and Abel and their story regarding the stronghold of jealousy? Cain was jealous because his brother Abel's offering was pleasing to the Lord while his offering was not. Cain's emotions did not stop at jealousy. His jealousy led to uncontrolled anger which led him to kill Abel over the incident. Had he just controlled his anger and let go of his jealousy, Cain wouldn't have killed his brother.

Righteous anger

It is critical that we discern that there is a <u>righteous</u> anger as well as the <u>unrighteous</u> anger that we have been discussing. God knew we would have anger—He had anger Himself. Jesus is our example of righteous anger. When He went into the temple (Mark 11:15) and saw how they were buying and selling instead of using it for a house of prayer, He overturned the tables. He felt indignation over the misuse of His Father's house, and righteously attacked that sin.

Righteous anger is a deep, justified anger and is the only anger allowed by God. It can be profitable if handled correctly. For example, I was at a women's exercise class in which secular music was being played. Usually it was not a problem. One day, however, a song came on that was absolutely vulgar and offensive. I felt that I had to say something out loud to the instructor while we were exercising. She knew that I was upset and put on another song. Afterwards, several of the women in the class came up to me and thanked me for my boldness as the song upset them, too. Later, I went to my instructor and told her privately that I wasn't angry with her, but with the male singer who was making women look like nothing more than sex objects. I didn't want to listen to that kind of music. She understood and apologized.

Righteous anger can be positive, but you must be diplomatic and not explosive. When you hear things being said or see things that go against God's Word, it is acceptable to diplomatically express your anger. Anger can be used as a good thing if you handle yourself correctly. Proverbs 15:18 MSG explains this, *Hot tempers start fights; a calm, cool spirit keeps the peace.*

Step One: Face your anger

Before you can begin to tackle the stronghold of anger, you first need to admit that your anger is a problem and needs to be healed. Anger is the result of unresolved issues. Do you have problems with road rage, or with blowing up, or with blurting out hurtful comments? Are you easily upset when no one else seems to be? These actions are not normal—to the world they are—but for a person who's under self-control from the Holy Spirit, those are not acceptable reactions.

You must recognize that feelings of rage are not appropriate. Blowing up at people who do not agree with your ideas is not healthy. Shouting and cursing at people who do things differently from the way you would like, like the other driver in the story at the beginning of this chapter, is destructive behavior. Even worse, becoming violent is totally unacceptable—you may hurt others and end up in jail, just like the woman in the chapter on jealousy who became enraged at her husband's affair. Additionally, if you continue to burn with anger about an offense and can never seem to let it go, you probably have a stronghold of anger. Don't give the devil a foothold in your life. You've got to face this stronghold and proceed in pulling it down.

In today's world, another aspect of anger to be aware of is with social media and digital technology. How many of you have seen social media arguments escalate into heated, disrespectful, seemingly endless jousts? How many of you have participated in them? Some people seem to stalk online threads just to post their latest jab at another person. Ranting seems to be dismissed as acceptable when you hide behind a phone or laptop. However, all of this behavior is contrary to God's standards and reflects uncontrolled anger.

Step Two: Find the root

As always, the next step in pulling down this stronghold is to get to the root. If your father or mother blew up over anything or everything, you could very easily have learned to imitate that behavior and think it to be normal. Some people have traumatic experiences that they've never been able to talk about or deal with. That suppressed hurt, pain, and frustration can cause anger.

There are many reasons why we may get angry, so it is important to try to identify the "root" of what triggers our anger. Below are a few of the most common reasons:

1. **Jealousy**—Anger, as we saw with Cain, can cause you to do and say things that are out of control. Such out-of-control anger can bring serious negative consequences in your life. You may need to pull down two strongholds, both jealousy and anger.

2. **Angry Families**—Being raised with an angry family can produce an angry person. If a child is allowed to have temper tantrums or express abnormal anger, he or she will continue with such behavior into adulthood. Being around angry people and being allowed to express your anger without consequences will make you think that anger is normal. Proverbs 29:11 contradicts this, *A [shortsighted] fool always loses his temper and displays his anger, But a wise man [uses self-control and] holds it back.*

3. **Impatience**—Sometimes when people can't get their way or when they want something right away and don't get it, they get angry. It is a constant temptation in this fast-paced world,

but God can give you supernatural patience. Some people have been spoiled, always getting their way. If this is the case with you, you need to look to God for patience—He has it in abundance.

4. **Unforgiveness and Bitterness**—These negative emotions can cause you to lash out at others because of what you feel inside. The Bible tells you how to avoid this behavior in Ephesians 4:26-27 MSG, *Go ahead and be angry. You do well to be angry—but don't use your anger as fuel for revenge. And don't stay angry. Don't go to bed angry. Don't give the Devil that kind of foothold in your life.* Anger held inside hurts and upsets you, causing you to do things and say things you later regret. When possible, try to talk the problem out with the other person. If for some reason talking to the other person isn't possible—such as when the person is your boss or when someone treats you badly or abuses you—talk to a friend. In Matthew 5:44, Jesus told us to pray for our enemies. I once worked at a place where I supervised a group of women who really resented me. One woman in particular always acted very angrily toward me. The circumstances were heightened by the fact that I was the only Christian in the office. One day, I asked the woman what the problem in the office was, and she lashed out at me saying, "You! You're the problem!" Well, I was furious, and I walked out of the building, intending to quit. Thank the Lord for Christian elders. When I talked to my spiritual couselor about the situation, he said, "You are not going to quit, and you will be going back tomorrow." He prayed for me to let go of all my anger and unforgiveness. His prayers helped, and I took my problems to the Lord, who then showed me that my job would purify me and help me change and grow into a better, stronger person. I was being put in a "melting pot" to bring up things in me that the Lord wanted to work on. The girls I worked with could be quite rude and hard to get along with. Even though I didn't want to be there, Jesus was showing me how to love and forgive through putting on the nature of Christ. I became determined to make the situation better. I prayed every day for my enemies at the job. I asked God to help me see them through His eyes and to treat them with His love. It was not easy, but

I did it (most of the time) and I began to see all of us change. At the end when I was leaving my job to move, my co-workers gave me a going-away party. These women no longer resented me, but actually cared that I was leaving. How different the situation would have ended if I had not let go of my anger and unforgiveness. The Lord can do great things in us if we give Him permission.

5. **Frustration**—Just as with my experience in the previously mentioned job, you will have circumstances in your life which will lead to frustration and anger. Ask God to give you peace instead of anger in order to walk in victory and to show the kind of love Jesus had.

6. **A chip on your shoulder from experiences you have gone through**—Many people who have suffered verbal, emotional, sexual, or physical abuse, and unfair treatment are easily angered because they are still wounded from their past experiences. The following story shows the problems that can arise when a person has a chip on his shoulder. I once had a student on a mission trip who was always easily angered and hard to be around. I finally confronted him. At first, he said he didn't see any problem with his behavior—that the problems we were experiencing were the fault of other people. I told him to go ask the Lord what He thought about it, and he came back to me and said he saw that it was his fault. After we talked, he began to pour out to me how mean and abusive his father had been. He still had much anger toward him for the angry way he was raised. Finally, I got him to see that his unhealed hurt over his past was triggering his anger. He agreed to forgive his father and let it go, thus he began to get free from the bondage of unforgiveness. His anger habit took some time to change, but when I saw him after the trip, I could see a change in him—and so could others. He said he felt he now had control over situations and that all his repressed anger toward his dad had been released. His life is an example to forgive and not seek revenge, as Romans 12:19 tells us, *Beloved, never avenge yourselves, but leave the way open for God's wrath (and His judicial righteousness); for it is written (in Scripture), "Vengeance is Mine, I will repay," says the Lord.*

7. **Strife**—Strife is repressed anger. People with strife issues are difficult to get along with, and the underlying reason is that they haven't dealt with their anger. They are angry at life, angry at themselves, and no matter what you do or say, they are very uncooperative.

8. **Unmet Needs**—Having ongoing unmet needs can produce anger. You have needs that can and should be met by those closest to you. When that does not happen, you feel angry. You must communicate your needs. However, you must realize that people will never be able to meet all your needs—only the Lord can truly satisfy your deepest needs for love. Ask the Lord to help you accept the things in life that you cannot change and to give you peace. Another important thing to consider is that not everyone expresses anger outwardly—many people are "passive aggressive." That means that while they seem compliant on the surface, inwardly they are defiant and angry. These people use the silent treatment or sulking to punish others and try to get their way. They say nothing, then after a while, they suddenly "blow up." This passive-aggressive behavior is not healthy. If you recognize this pattern in your life, you need to be open and communicate your feelings instead of holding it all in. Deal with your feelings when you are upset.

Step Three: Renewing your mind and conquering anger

After admitting your problem and going to the Lord to understand the cause, you're ready to move on to the third step of renewing your mind to God's Word and being set free. These seven things can help you remain free from the bondage of anger.

1. <u>Realize you have a tendency to react in anger</u>. Ecclesiastes 7:9 MSG says, *Don't be quick to fly off the handle. Anger boomerangs. You can spot a fool by the lumps on his head.* Many people see their outbursts, such as yelling, as a normal way to handle their feelings, but the Bible does not agree.

2. <u>Pause before you answer</u> when you are in a heated argument. Instead of reacting out of your soul (where your emotions are

stored), act on the Word of God. Take the time to pause and allow the Lord to bring scripture to your mind and avoid speaking in anger.

3. <u>Meditate on Scripture</u>. Many people change effortlessly after meditating on scriptures. Focus on the scriptures which deal with anger and peace, such as Colossians 3:15 NIV, *Let the peace of Christ rule in your hearts, since as members of one body you were called to peace. And be thankful.* Two additional scriptures that can help you are Psalm 37:8 NIV, *Refrain from anger and turn from wrath; do not fret—it only leads to evil,* and Ephesians 4:26 KJV, *Be angry and sin not: let not the sun go down upon your wrath.* Go over the scriptures mentioned throughout this chapter to find the peace you need. Ask God to make these scriptures become your mindset and to change you from your previous mindset of always blowing up.

4. <u>Be quick to forgive</u>. You cannot feed and nurture anger against someone. Give it to God. He is your example to always forgive others, instead of fueling anger.

5. <u>Talk it out with God or share it with someone—pray and ask God to take the anger</u>. Ephesians 4:31 NIV tells us, *Get rid of all bitterness, rage, and anger, brawling and slander, along with every form of malice.*

6. <u>One person you can get angry with is Satan</u>. He is the one who is always using people to provoke you to anger. Just like you know it is impossible that offenses will come, it is the same for anger. Just be sure you direct your anger toward the real enemy, rather than toward one another.

Self-evaluation questions

To help you understand if you have a stronghold of anger, ask yourself these questions:

- Do I find myself "blowing up" and getting frustrated or angry with everyday situations?

- Do I struggle to control feelings of anger?

- Do I tend to become obsessed with online arguments and disregard courteous behavior during these arguments?

- Is my anger tied to other negative emotions, such as jealousy, impatience, unforgiveness, or strife?

- Am I full of resentment and bitterness because of past offenses toward me? Do I let anger continually resurface when I think about an offense I've experienced?

- Do I desire to exact revenge on people who have hurt me?

- Do I now have—or I ever had—ongoing unmet needs that left me with emotional scars?

- Did I grow up in an angry family, and am I imitating that behavior?

- Do I hold my feelings in, harboring offense and anger, leading me to passive-aggressive behavior, such as sulking, gossip, and the silent treatment?

Scriptures to pull down the stronghold of anger

Renew your mind and get freedom from anger with these scriptures:

Refrain from anger and turn from wrath; do not fret—it leads only to evil. —Psalm 37:8

Hot tempers start fights; a calm, cool spirit keeps the peace. —Proverbs 15:18 MSG

Go ahead and be angry. You do well to be angry, but don't use your anger as fuel for revenge. And don't stay angry. Don't go to bed angry. Don't

give the Devil that kind of foothold in your life. —Ephesians 4:26-27 MSG (This scripture is specific to passive aggressiveness.)

Beloved, never avenge yourselves, but leave the way open for God's wrath; for it is written, "Vengeance is Mine, I will repay," says the Lord. —Romans 12:19

Let all bitterness and wrath and anger and clamor [perpetual animosity, resentment, strife, fault-finding] and slander be put away from you, along with every kind of malice [all spitefulness, verbal abuse, malevolence]. —Ephesians 4:31

Don't be quick to fly off the handle. Anger boomerangs. You can spot a fool by the lumps on his head. —Ecclesiastes 7:9 MSG

Let the peace of Christ [the inner calm of one who walks daily with Him] be the controlling factor in your hearts [deciding and settling questions that arise]. To this peace indeed you were called as members in one body [of believers]. And be thankful [to God always]. —Colossians 3:15

Conclusion

It is imperative that we realize that the non-Christian world's behavior and thinking are different from the behavior and thinking of a Christian. The Bible says that we live in the world but are not of the world. We have to train ourselves to not model what the world thinks or how the world acts. The people in the world are lost, like sheep without a shepherd. Before we were saved, we walked and talked like the unsaved world. When we accepted Jesus as our savior, everything changed. We were transformed from the darkness into the light. Second Corinthians 4:4 tells us that Satan has blinded the unbeliever's mind: *the god of this world [Satan] has blinded the minds of the unbelieving to prevent them from seeing the illuminating light of the gospel of the glory of Christ, who is the image of God.* As believers, we have now been given the ability to see and understand spiritual truths because of the finished work of Jesus.

I remember when I was born again at age twenty-eight, I thought to myself, "It's like someone woke me up and took the blinders off my eyes." Now that I was in relationship with Jesus, life made sense. I realized after beginning to read the Bible that I had been living the opposite of how the Lord created me to live to be happy. No wonder things weren't going well and I felt empty. Once I made Jesus my Lord and my Everything, I felt loved and complete. My search was over. What I was looking for to make me happy and satisfied was not a career, marriage, and other material things, but it was all found in Him.

Let's look at a summary of the sixteen strongholds covered in this book. You can be deceived into thinking that these are a normal, uncontrollable part of who you are, versus what the Bible says about how the Lord wants you to act or think:

Normal for the World	Normal for Christians
Fear, worry, anxiety	Trusting God to take care of us, then rest and peace will come
Rejection, low self-esteem, guilt, shame	Godly confidence, new self-image, freedom from guitl and shame
Jealousy	Contentment
Unforgiveness and bitterness	God's love and forgiveness
Lust and sexual defilement	Sexual purity
Pride, rebellion, lying	Humility, submission, truthfulness
Anger	Even temper, self-control, God's patience

You may look at the Christian's normal behavior, emotion, and thinking list and say it looks impossible to attain. However, you must always remember that you are not alone now and have an Abba Father who loves you and wants to heal and change you. You can't do it yourself, but if you give Him your permission and acknowledge that you want a particular thought or action to be changed or taken from your life, He will help you do it. Just as the Lord can physically heal you, so can He heal you spiritually and emotionally. Remember you are three parts—body, soul, and spirit. All parts affect each other. Problems in your soul can result in physical ailments. The story below illustrates this:

At one point in my life, I had a serious disease which got worse each year. I ended up in the hospital for a month. When I was released, one of the top specialists in my disease told me that the illness was incurable and that I would have to live with it for the rest of my life. The disease affected my mind as well as my body and I was miserable. After I was born again and began to believe that I could be healed, I started praying for my body to be healed. Nothing was happening. Finally, I asked the Lord, "Why?" I clearly heard Him say, "You are so concerned about your physical healing, but what about the soulical healing that you need for all those negative emotions and habits?" God began to show me many of the strongholds in this book and told me that He wanted to heal my soul—my mind, will, and emotions.

Giving up those negative thought patterns and emotions looked so hard, but I swallowed my pride and told God I was ready, one stronghold at a time. As I did my part—such as forgiving my parents and even writing them a letter asking them to forgive me for all the bitterness I had for being sent to boarding school—I began to see signs of a physical healing. It took time, however.

Life consists of two types of actions. We all have things that we <u>get</u> to do and things we <u>have</u> to do. What I had to do—pulling down my multiple strongholds was the latter category. Was it easy? No! Did I want to exchange some of my bad fruit for good fruit? No, but I did it anyway. Almost two years later, not only did I start to talk and act like a new creature in Christ, but my incurable disease was completely healed! It was shortly afterwards that I ended up being with my soon-to-be husband. He told me that I looked and acted differently from when he had first met me several years earlier. He even said he really didn't even like me when he first met me, but then, after several years, I was the one he wanted to marry. What a miracle the Lord did in me, with my cooperation. I can't emphasize this enough—it's up to you to make the changes you need to make.

God's fruits of the spirit are these: *love (unselfish concern for others), joy, (inner) peace, patience, kindness, goodness, faithfulness, gentleness, and self-control.* (Galatians 5:22) Some of Satan's fruits are these: Instead of <u>love</u>, he gives us unforgiveness and offense. Instead of <u>joy</u>, he gives us rejection, guilt, and shame. Instead of <u>peace</u>, Satan gives us fear, anxiety, and worry. Instead of <u>patience</u>, Satan gives us anger and rebellion. Instead of <u>kindness</u>, <u>goodness</u>, and <u>gentleness</u>, he gives us jealousy and pride. Instead of

<u>faithfulness</u>, he gives us rebellion and lying. Instead of <u>self-control</u>, he gives us lust and sexual impurities. If you allow bad fruit to grow in your life, they may soon become the strongholds discussed in this book.

God wants to break the chains (strongholds) Satan has wrapped around you. These hidden sins or bad fruit in your life can only be dealt with if you are willing to expose them. As you surrender your will and let the Word begin to wash out your old mindsets (Ephesians 5:26), delighting yourself in the Lord (Psalm 37), He will begin to give you His desires on how to live, instead of yours. According to 2 Corinthians 10, your weapons to do this are not mere human weapons, but mighty with God who will help you overthrow and destroy your strongholds and take the thoughts and actions captive to the way He wants you to think and act.

You can walk away from the lies that the enemy and the world have fed you about how you should act and think. Now, instead, you can begin to walk according to how the Bible—your <u>B</u>asic <u>I</u>nstruction <u>B</u>efore <u>L</u>eaving <u>E</u>arth—teaches you.

Your will and determination to be changed and renewing your mind by reading and doing His Word are an unbeatable duo!

Here are some comforting words, "A Love Letter from God to You" to help you on your way to being no longer bound:

My Child,
You may not know me, but I know everything about you. (Psalm 139:1)
I know when you sit down and when you rise up. (Psalm 139:2)
I am familiar with all your ways. (Psalm 139:3).
Even the very hairs on your head are numbered. (Matthew 10:29-31)
For you were made in my image. (Genesis 1:27)
In me you live and move and have your being. (Acts 17:28)
For you are my offspring. (Acts 17:28)
I knew you even before you were conceived. (Jeremiah 1:4-5)
I chose you when I planned creation. (Ephesians 1:11-12)
You were not a mistake, for all your days are written in my book. (Psalm 139:15-16)

*I determined the exact time of your birth and where you would live.
(Acts 17:26)
You are fearfully and wonderfully made. (Psalm 139:14)
I knit you together in your mother's womb. (Psalm 139:13)
And brought you forth on the day you were born. (Psalm 71:6)
I have been misrepresented by those who don't know me. (John 8:41-44)
I am not distant and angry but am the complete expression of love
(1 John 4:16)
And it is my desire to lavish my love on you. (1 John 3:1)
Simply because you are my child and I am your Father. (1 John 3:1)
I offer you more than your earthly father ever could. (Matthew 7:11)
For I am the perfect father. (Matthew 5:48)
Every good gift that you receive comes from my hand. (James 1:17)
For I am your provider and I meet all your needs. (Matthew 6:31-33)
My plan for your future has always been filled with hope. (Jeremiah 29:11)
Because I love you with an everlasting love. (Jeremiah 31:3)
My thoughts toward you are countless as the sand on the seashore.
(Psalm 139:17-18)
And I rejoice over you with singing. (Zephaniah 3:17)
I will never stop doing good to you. (Jeremiah 32:40)
For you are my treasured possession. (Exodus 19:5)
I desire to establish you with all my heart and all my soul. (Jeremiah 32:41)
And I want to show you great and marvelous things. (Jeremiah 33:3)
If you seek me with all your heart, you will find me. (Deuteronomy 4:29)
Delight in me and I will give you the desires of your heart. (Psalm 37:4)
For it is I who gave you those desires. (Philippians 2:13)
I am able to do more for you than you could possibly imagine.
(Ephesians 3:20)
For I am your greatest encourager. (2 Thessalonians 2:16-17)
I am also the Father who comforts you in all your troubles.
(2 Corinthians 1:3-4)
When you are brokenhearted, I am close to you. (Psalm 34:18)
As a shepherd carries a lamb, I have carried you close to my heart.
(Isaiah 40:11)
One day I will wipe away every tear from your eyes. (Revelation 21:3-4)
And I'll take away all the pain you have suffered on this earth.
(Revelation 21:3-4)
I am your Father, and I love you even as I love my son, Jesus. (John 17:23)
For in Jesus, my love for you is revealed. (John 17:26)
He is the exact representation of my being. (Hebrews 1:3)*

He came to demonstrate that I am for you, not against you. (Romans 8:31)
And to tell you that I am not counting your sins. (2 Corinthians 5:18-19)
Jesus died so that you and I could be reconciled. (2 Corinthians 5:18-19)
His death was the ultimate expression of my love for you. (1 John 4:10)
I gave up everything I loved that I might gain your love. (Romans 8:31-32)
If you receive the gift of my son Jesus, you receive me. (1 John 2:23)
And nothing will ever separate you from my love again. (Romans 8:38-39)
Come home and I'll throw the biggest party heaven has ever seen.
(Luke 15:7)
I have always been Father and will always be Father. (Ephesians 3:14-15)
My question is ... Will you be my child? (John 1:12-13)
I am waiting for you. (Luke 15:11-32)
Love,
Your Dad
Almighty God

Finally, here are some words to empower you from Psalm 107:13-16 NIV: Then they cried to the Lord in their trouble, and he saved them from their distress. He brought them out of darkness, the utter darkness, and <u>broke away their chains</u>. Let them give thanks to the Lord for his unfailing love and his wonderful deeds for mankind, for he breaks down gates of bronze and cuts through bars of iron.

Teach All Nations Mission

Teach All Nations Mission (TAN) is a global evangelical educational ministry birthed from the teaching ministries of Delron and Peggy Shirley. The name for Teach All Nations Mission was chosen to carefully indicate the exact heart of the Shirleys' mission. TAN's commitment is to establish a solid foundation in national pastors and leaders so they can help enrich their people. This vision is being accomplished by holding national leadership conferences and publishing and distributing Christian teaching materials in English and their local languages.

Someone accurately observed concerning the revival occurring in many parts of our world today that it is a mile wide but only an inch deep – the result of energetic evangelism by both missionaries and local Christians. Sadly, there is a marked shortage of teachers who are taking the next step in fulfilling our Lord's directive to teach them how to observe all that He has commanded. Therefore, Teach All Nations Mission has literally taken the words of Christ from Matthew 28:19, "Teach all nations," as its motto and mission statement.

TAN's commitment is to deepen that revival by training the pastors and leaders who then go back and strengthen their congregations. TAN pays for the travel and lodging of handpicked leaders because Delron and Peggy want to invest into their lives but know that these third-world saints could never afford to come at their own expense. TAN always provides the meals for all the guests during these conferences. The ministry also furnishes solid Christian literature in their local language or in English for those who understand the language.

Delron and Peggy realize that the challenge is much bigger than what they can accomplish in person; therefore, they have determined to expand the scope of their vision. One area of expansion includes a scholarship fund that will allow selected individuals to obtain formal education in solid Christian colleges and Bible schools or through correspondence courses. The ministry has also assisted in building a Christian school in

Zimbabwe and a Bible college in Nepal. Additionally, Teach All Nations assists the pastors and leaders they work with in times of need such as the tsunami in Sri Lanka, the hurricane in Belize, and the earthquake in Nepal.

Books by Delron & Peggy Shirley

Available at:
teachallnationsmission.com

Bingo, a Fresh Look at Grace
Christmas Thoughts
Cornerstones of Faith
Daily Bible Study Series (Five-Volume Set)
Daily Ditties from Delron's Desk
(Seven Volumes Available)
Lessons from the Life of David
The Great Commission – DOABLE
Doctor Livingstone, I Presume
Don't Leave Home Without It
Finally, My Brethren
Going Deeper in Jesus
The IN Factors
In This Sign Conquer
Interface
Israel, Key to Human Destiny
The Last Enemy
Lessons Along the Way
Living for the End Times
Maturing into the Full Stature of Jesus Christ
Maximum Impact
No Longer Bound
The Non-Conformer's Trilogy
Of Kings and Prophets
Passion for the Harvest
People Who Make A Difference
Positioned for Blessing and Power
Problem People of the Bible
Seeds and Harvest
The Seventh Man at the Well
So Send I You
So, You Wanna be a Preacher

Thirty-, Sixty-, One-Hundred-Fold
Tread Marks
Turning the World Upside Down and Back Again
Verse for the Day (Four Volumes Available)
Women for the Harvest
You'll be Darned to Heck if You Don't Believe in Gosh
Your Home Can Survive in the 21st Century

Printed in the USA
CPSIA information can be obtained
at www.ICGtesting.com
JSHW021222160923
48244JS00004B/93